# "Then **Morton** Said to **Elway**..."

## *The Best Denver Broncos Football Stories Ever Told*

Craig Morton and Adrian Dater

TRIUMPH
BOOKS

Library of Congress Cataloging-in-Publication Data

Morton, Craig, 1943–
Then Morton said to Elway—: the best Denver Broncos football stories ever told / Craig Morton and Adrian Dater.
     p. cm.
  ISBN-13: 978-1-60078-121-6
  ISBN-10: 1-60078-121-7
1. Denver Broncos (Football team)—History. I. Dater, Adrian. II. Title III. Title: Best Denver Bronco stories ever told
  GV956.D37M67 2008
  796.332'640978883—dc22

                              2008014142

This book is available in quantity at special discounts for your group or organization. For further information, contact:

**Triumph Books**
542 South Dearborn Street
Suite 750
Chicago, Illinois 60605
(312) 939-3330
Fax (312) 663-3557

Printed in U.S.A.
ISBN: 978-1-60078-121-6
Design by Patricia Frey
Photos courtesy of Getty Images unless otherwise indicated.

# table of
## contents

# preface

This book is primarily about a man who I didn't know at all when I started writing it. Sure, I knew *of* Craig Morton, but I had no idea about the real person. Thanks to Alexander Graham Bell's invention and one glorious afternoon spent at a restaurant overlooking the sparkling Pacific Ocean, I got to know Larry Craig Morton. I am glad for having had the opportunity.

Time and again, over several months of talking to him, I heard about what a great guy so-and-so was and what great times were had together. This was not delusion or spin, I would soon learn. All the people Morton called friends called him one right back.

Of all the things Craig Morton is and has been in life, perfect is not one. Many of his foibles are detailed in the pages ahead.

But they say wisdom comes from humility, so today Morton is a very wise man. His has been a full life—and that means success, failure, joy, and pain. He has been a "brash idiot" and a "humble old man." He knows what buying a brand-new Jaguar feels like and the embarrassment of filing for bankruptcy. He knows what it feels like to be handed a Super Bowl championship ring and to fail miserably in football's biggest game. He knows the miracle of fatherhood and the blackness of divorce.

This is not a pure biography. It is a collection of memories, his primarily, but also those of his many teammates. The word *teammate*, to Morton, means friend, so mainly it's a story about friends.

It is also a snapshot look at one of football's greatest teams, the Denver Broncos. Entering 2008, the Broncos were the only NFL team with more Super Bowl appearances (six) than Hall of Fame players (four). Only two HOF players, John Elway and Gary Zimmerman, spent more than one year with the team. There is plenty of injustice in that, but it can't dim what has been a marvelous team history. The Broncos helped turn a Dusty Old Cow Town into an internationally renowned city that hosted a pope, a Democratic National Convention, and even one cast of MTV's show *The Real World.*

Craig Morton had something to do with that. He quarterbacked the Broncos to their first Super Bowl in 1978, a team that will forever be known as the Orange Crush. Today, the No. 7 jersey of the Broncos is retired, instantly recognized as belonging to Elway, Morton's successor.

But there are still many hardcore Broncomaniacs who proudly wear a No. 7 jersey with the name Morton on the back. To those fans, and hopefully many other casual ones, this book is a look inside that original No. 7. Or, as the label on a bottle of Jack Daniels says: "Old No. 7." There is no shortage of irony there, as you'll soon see.

Overall, this story is about "a gentleman," as Morton's good friend Dan Reeves called him. Not a saint, or a choirboy, but rather a gentle man, who chose a life in a rough profession and lived to tell about it.

—Adrian Dater

# acknowledgments

To all of you who have touched my life, I thank you very much. I have been so privileged to know the best of the best. My friends are my soul and without their influence and lessons learned (some easy, some more difficult), I would have had very little success. I can't name all of you but please know that you have brought me the joy, success, and happiness we all strive to have.

—Craig Morton

I would like to, first of all, thank Craig Morton for his generous time and effort in making this book possible. Without him, there is no book. Also thanks to his wife, Kym, for her advice on getting over a particularly awful cold during the writing process.

Also thanks to the following former players and coaches for their time and insight: Jim Turner, Mark Schlereth, Frank Tripucka, Jason Elam, Rod Smith, Roger Staubach, Randy Gradishar, Billy Thompson, Dan Reeves, Marlin Briscoe, and Rich Karlis.

Thanks to the following media friends and colleagues for their insight: Woody Paige, Mark Kiszla, Terry Frei, Sandy Clough, and Gary Miller.

Thanks to Dallas Cowboys fan nonpareil Chris Spaulding for his insights into the teams of the 1960s and '70s.

Thanks to my bosses at *The Denver Post* for allowing me the privilege of writing the book, and to the librarians at the paper for helping me pore over the archives.

Thanks to the publications and other media sources mentioned in the text for material that contributed to this book.

Thanks to my wife, Heidi, and son, Thomas Alan Michael, for allowing me to sneak away to the computer too many times.

—Adrian Dater

# introduction

A lot of football fans, when they remember the career of quarterback Craig Morton, recall only his years as a Denver Bronco. And why not? They were probably the best and most exciting of his 18-year NFL career.

But not many, other than fervent Morton fans, remember that he played 12 years previously in the league with the Dallas Cowboys and the New York Giants. He led the Cowboys to their first Super Bowl in 1971, losing a tough 16–13 decision to the Baltimore Colts; got a Super Bowl ring with the victorious Cowboys in the next Super Bowl; and was the valiant quarterback on some otherwise bad Giants teams from 1974 to 1976.

In April 1977, Morton was traded by the Giants to the Broncos in a deal that sent quarterback Steve Ramsey to New York.

By this point in his career, Morton was considered as possibly on his last football legs. Those legs weren't in such great shape. His body was battered in his time with the Giants, a team with a porous offensive line that left Morton feeling like he was the last fighter standing at the Alamo.

But instead of a last year or two in the literal and figurative twilight of the Rocky Mountains, Morton thrust himself, his team, and his city into the brightest spotlight of pro football.

The 1977 Broncos would go on to their first Super Bowl with Morton leading the way. He would spend another five seasons in Denver, and although another Super Bowl wasn't in the cards, he played in numerous unforgettable games that live on in Broncos history.

When football fans in Denver today remember their quarterback who wore the No. 7, most naturally think of Hall of Fame player John Elway, the Duke of Denver. Elway succeeded Morton in 1983 and played until 1998, winning Super Bowls his last two years as a player.

But there are still many Broncos fans who think of Morton as the real No. 7. While Elway retired the number when he quit as a Bronco, a No. 7 also hangs next to Morton's name in the Broncos' official Ring of Fame at Invesco Field located at Mile High Stadium.

Craig Morton was the first quarterback in Broncos history to have the entire city idolize his every move. He gave the locals, who'd suffered through much awful football since the team's 1960 American Football League inception, their first taste of big-time success.

Never a very mobile quarterback, Morton had a gunslinger's arm and mentality. He had one of the stronger throwing arms in NFL history, certainly of his era. He was also one of the toughest players. A pure pocket passer, Morton took the kind of physical punishment that probably would have been too much for most of his contemporaries to endure. Morton had an amazing ability to play through pain. During the AFC Championship Game in 1977 against Oakland, his entire left leg and hip were literally black with congealed blood.

Morton took some terrific beatings, especially in his days with the Giants. His response was almost always the same: he'd just get right back up and call the next play.

This book is a collection of Morton's memories of his Denver playing years. A few other memories are sprinkled in from his time with the Giants and Cowboys. This book also includes little-known facts about his life, pre- and post-football. Mistakes? Yeah, Morton has made a few, and he doesn't shy away from detailing some of them here. It is story of a man who grew up picking apricots and prunes in the quiet orchards of Northern California and later became the leader of a team nicknamed the Orange Crush.

# chapter 1
# From the Big Apple to a Cow Town

*"So, McVay calls and tells me, 'We're really sorry, Craig, but we've traded your rights to the Denver Broncos.'*
*"'Well', I said, 'You've got to be kidding me? That's GREAT!'*

—Craig Morton

New York City was quite an interesting place to be in the late '70s. It was a time marked by terror, with a serial killer nicknamed Son of Sam on the loose. It was time when the city's coffers were literally empty, with high unemployment and inflation. It was a time when the New York Yankees were nicknamed 'The Bronx Zoo' from all its colorful characters, including a brash owner named George Steinbrenner.

Furthermore, one of the city's football teams, the New York Giants, didn't add much excitement to the mix. The Giants were awful. This once-proud franchise was reduced to playing in whatever venue might take them, which in the mid-1970s included the Yale Bowl in Connecticut, Yankee Stadium, and Shea Stadium. A new stadium was under construction for the Giants, slated to open in 1976, but it wasn't in New York City. It was in New Jersey, on a piece of cheap marshland called the Meadowlands.

From 1974 to 1976, the Giants' quarterback was Craig Morton. He was obtained by New York in a trade with Dallas. Despite being in his early thirties, Morton thought his best playing days were ahead of him. In his early years with the Cowboys he didn't play much, as he was the backup to Don Meredith and he often split time with Roger Staubach in the later ones.

But as Morton would soon realize, playing for the Giants was nearly a career killer. He played a lot, sure, but much of his time in a Giants uniform was spent trying not to get the holy Hell kicked out of him.

"I remember I was traded by the Giants in April of 1977, and everybody thought I was about washed up because we were such a bad team. The funny thing is, when I was traded by Dallas to the Giants, I had said I just had to get out of Dallas, because with Roger (Staubach) and I there, it just wasn't going to work. At first, it was going to (be) Roger that went, then in the middle of the last season there, I just asked to be traded. I thought I was going to the 49ers, but at the last minute they traded me to the Giants for a No. 1 draft choice, who turned out to be Randy White. So that was a good trade for them.

*Craig Morton began his NFL career in 1965 with the Dallas Cowboys, before being traded to the New York Giants in 1974, then finally to Denver to be the Broncos quarterback in 1977.* Photo courtesy of Wirelmages.

"The first day I walked into the Giants Stadium, it wasn't a particularly good time in the city. That's when they were running out of money, and President Ford had to bail them out. I had a great time in New York, as far as being a bachelor and all that, but I remember getting to LaGuardia and the guy from the Giants was late picking me up, and I said, 'What in the world have I done? Is this the dumbest-ass move I've ever made, or what? You should have kept your mouth shut.'

"With the Giants, the first day I got there, I learned you had to get there early. Because, unlike the Cowboys, who always had all your gear in your locker and it was always perfect and real professional, the Giants had three stacks of clothes. One was a stack of socks, one was a sack of jocks, and one was a stack of T-shirts. You had to get there early to get any socks that would stay up, any jocks that weren't broken, and a shirt that wasn't shrunk up around your belly button.

"I just said to myself 'you've really made a great decision to call home here,' because this is not a good organization. We played at Yankee Stadium, we played at the Yale Bowl, we played at Shea Stadium, then we opened Giants Stadium. And we weren't good at any place we played.

"After the last season (1976), our coach, Bill Arnsparger, was fired. So, I get a call from John McVay, who was the interim coach. I didn't know what was going to happen, but I didn't want to go back to New York. The people didn't like me there; they were cursing and yelling at me. I used to get my friends around me and we'd run to my car, because we didn't have a protected area to park in those days. But my friends were faster than I was and the

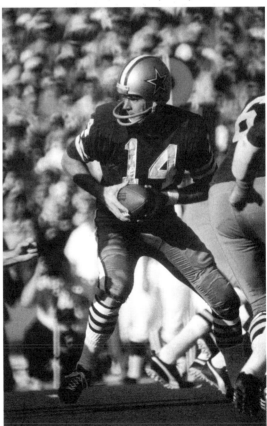

*Morton shared the Cowboys quarterback spotlight with fellow teammate and future Hall of Famer Roger Staubach. The two remain friends despite vying for the same quarterback position in the early 1970s.*
Photo courtesy of WireImages.

fans would catch up with me, and let me have it. It was just horrible, not a good deal *at all*.

"So, McVay calls and tells me, 'We're really sorry, Craig, but we've traded your rights to the Denver Broncos.'

"'Well', I said, 'You've got to be kidding me? That's GREAT!' Because, one of my last games with the Giants was against the Broncos, and in preparation for playing them, I found (out) that they were already a pretty good team. They had a great defense. Their offense wasn't so good, but they didn't make a lot of mistakes.

"And, another great thing was that a friend, Johnny Walker, and I had a place up in Aspen that we used to go to in all the off-seasons. So, I'd known Denver and loved it. I thought the Broncos had potential. So, I just thought, 'God, this is great.' And, of course, they had a new coach in Denver, Red Miller. Denver took my contract from the Giants, and it was a good little contract. I think I was making $100,000 to $150,000 a year at the time, I can't quite remember which. But it was good money. And, the thing is, I wasn't assured of having a job in Denver. They already had Craig Penrose and Norris Weese as quarterbacks, and they also brought in Steve Spurrier.

"But I had a good feeling about things, from the first moment I walked in the locker room. That first time, I see this big old guy sitting at the end of the room. It was Lyle Alzado. I knew him by name...and from him just kicking my ass in the game we played. And I went up to him and he says, 'Craig Morton—NOW we can win a championship.' So that made me feel that, hey, maybe somebody's on my side here.

"But the funny thing was, in my first training up, my first roommate was Craig Penrose. So, here we are, both wanting the same job. And Spurrier was there, too. He'd had a pretty good career to that point. Not great, but pretty good. So, there was competition for the job, but not to the point where I thought I was in danger of not getting the starting job. But me and Penrose would hang out at the local bars in Fort Collins, and they had a fan poll one night on one of the stations about who should get the starting job. Penrose and I were looking up at the screen and Penrose had the majority of the votes, and I had, like, 6 percent. And I said, 'Boy, I'm still a piece of crap.'"

## The Old Man's Still Got It

Despite the bad few seasons in New York, and a body that was starting to resemble a '53 Chevy on Demolition Derby Day, Morton hadn't given up on himself, probably because he knew he still had a gun for an arm.

In NFL history, Morton's arm compares favorably to most of the greats who got considerably more publicity and trophy hardware. Morton said that when he was growing up in California, he could actually throw a football faster than a baseball!

But after 12 years in the NFL, Morton's knees started deteriorating and his somewhat pigeon-toed walk would become a source of locker-room humor throughout his career. Through it all, Morton always had that gunslinger's arm, and that's why he entered the 1977 season with his new team's confidence. If nothing else, Morton was just happy to be in a new place.

"As training camp got started and went on, I knew I could still play in the league and be effective. I had just wanted to be on a better team, one with a good defense, and I knew this team had one. I was just so happy to be out of the Giants organization by then. There were no more fights everywhere, even on the way to the locker room after a practice or a game like we had there. It was a joke.

"But in Denver, I started feeling good about things again. I always had a great arm, and it was still there. Mentally, I could also play no matter how much I was hurt. I always thought, 'Nothing can hurt me.' I'd played with as much pain as anybody could play with. But through all that, I always had a strong arm. And with Denver, I knew I was going to be able to use it, but not have to throw 40 times a game because we had no running game. I could throw when I needed to, I had a feeling, and I just thought, 'This is going to work out here.'"

## New Coach For A New Quarterback

After the 1976 season, in which the Broncos went a franchise best 9–5, head coach John Ralston was fired. A so-called Gang of 12 contingent of veteran players supposedly went to upper management to say they couldn't play for Ralston anymore. It remains somewhat in dispute just who the mutineers were, but it has been safely established that star defensive lineman Lyle Alzado was a ringleader.

Some players saw Ralston, a former Stanford coach, as too much of a college-level coach. He wanted his players to hold hands in huddles. He was considered just too much of a sis-boom-bah, rah-rah kind of guy who didn't understand the mentality of the professional players. The pros left that kind of stuff behind the minute they started getting paychecks and non-guaranteed contracts.

In his place came Robert "Red" Miller. Miller was lured away as offensive coordinator from a fine New England Patriots team—one that might have gone to the Super Bowl in 1976 if not for a controversial roughing-the-passer call in a playoff game at Oakland. That gave the Raiders a second chance on a game-winning drive. Miller worked previously as an assistant with the Broncos in the 1960s, even during the team's vertically striped socks days. The look was so ugly they were named the third-worst-looking uniforms in pro sports history by ESPN.com. Only beating them on the list were the Chicago White Sox's wide-collared shirts, and the occasional short pants of the Bill Veeck-owned 1970s teams, which were voted the ugliest of any team sport. The ugliest overall was judged to be the all-white unitard worn by tennis player Anne White at the 1985 Wimbledon tournament.

Miller, a former Golden Gloves regional boxing champ in Illinois, was an energetic, rah-rah kind of coach, like Ralston. However, Miller earned the players' respect because of his "take no shit" personality, and because he wasn't afraid to get in the trenches with his own players. He was even known to have wrestled many of them in the locker room.

*The vertical striped socks helped name the Broncos the third-worst-looking uniforms in pro sports history by ESPN.com.* Photo courtesy of Wirelmages.

"John Ralston, I think, had pretty much been in control of all football operations when he was there, and he put together a great core of teammates. But he lacked the key ingredients, namely, a top quarterback, and I guess they wanted a change. But he certainly showed that he was a great judge of talent in his football career.

"But I liked Red right away. I'd played against his New England teams, and maybe he knew I was old enough or smart enough not to make a lot of mistakes. Red came in with this amazing energy. He was a real player's coach, and he just wanted to have fun but work really hard, too. He knew there was something special there."

"The first thing Red did was try to form a level of togetherness among the team. Before, not many guys lived in town. Everybody was all spread apart and there wasn't that cohesiveness, and Red wanted us to all try to live near each other. Red really wanted us to believe that we could win a championship together. Before, I don't think people really did. They thought we had a good enough defense, because they had such great leaders with guys like Randy Gradishar, Billy Thompson, Barney Chavous, Louis Wright, and Lyle.

"Red just kind of reaffirmed to them that, 'yeah, we are good enough to win' and he also had such a great coaching staff around him. Babe Parilli was my quarterback coach, and he was one of the great coaches of all time.

"A few things really stick out from my first training camp with Denver: One, I remember when we had a center named Bobby Maples, and he was getting old, but still a very talented guy. But there was a guy named Mike Montler, who turned out to be our starting center, who bicycled up from Boulder to Fort Collins. He was with Buffalo at the time, but he just biked up to our camp. I think Red was so overcome and impressed that Montler would come all the way up there and say he wanted to play there, that somehow we got him. Red traded for him.

"Another one was, at the first practice, he had us all run a mile. That was it. But here I was, coming from sea level, now at about 6,000 feet above it, or whatever it was. I wasn't in bad shape, and I thought, 'no problem.' I mean, we died. It was one of the hardest things I've ever had to do. It was a joke. I could see a look on Red's face like, 'Welcome to Colorado.' I think what he was trying to convey to us and guys like me was, 'The way you're feeling now, it's going to stay that way and you know how far you have to go, especially for you guys that don't live here. If you're going to play here, you're going to have to live here.' At the end, it did work, because I think 95 percent of our guys lived there year-round."

## The New Game Plan

While Morton had three other quarterbacks to beat out in his first Broncos training camp, there never was much doubt he'd get the starting job.

He'd had too much experience and his arm was still good enough to convince Miller the job was his. Miller didn't need a guy to throw for 300 yards a game. All he wanted, Morton soon would learn, was for his quarterback not to turn the ball over and get just enough on the scoreboard for what he believed would be a dominant defense.

He was right. It wouldn't be long before Denver's defense would be immortalized with the nickname "The Orange Crush."

"Red's whole deal was, 'We play to our defense.' He said, 'We will score. But if we can eliminate mistakes offensively, we have a great shot at winning.' Well, I'd always known that. But it's one thing to say it and another to have the kind of defense to be willing to punt the ball away, to play for good field position and just not throw any interceptions and avoid the sack, and wait for the next go-around when you'll get good field position.

"It took a little while to prove that, but Red was proven right. And I knew I could be that right quarterback for him, with that kind of game plan.

"I knew I could beat those guys out, but the guy who did concern me was Spurrier, because he had such an amazing grasp for the game. I'm sure that's why he became such a great coach. But they ended up cutting Spurrier, and keeping the young guys (Penrose and Weese). I guess they didn't want just old guys, because I was 34. I wanted to be that starting quarterback more than anything.

"I've always been able to compartmentalize things, to know what's important. I just remember being confident that I had what I needed to be successful for Red. And we all started to really respond to him. He was great, because he would always screw around with players, have fun with them, especially linemen.

"He'd come in the locker room and just go berserk with cheers and he'd go up and give guys forearms, and guys would think, 'what the hell am I supposed to do? Am I supposed to give a forearm back?' Then he'd get everybody in a circle and pick the biggest guy out and he'd start wrestling with them. And he'd kick anybody's ass. Everybody was afraid of 'who's he going to choose this week?' You'd see guys running in the bathroom. He'd just say, 'Come on! Get your ass out here, let's go.' I never saw him go after Alzado, though. I don't think he was that dumb.

"But guys respected him, because he showed he'd get his nose dirty with his own players. If he wanted to show something he wanted done on the line or something, he'd get right in there with no pads on and get all roughed up and have blood coming from his forehead or something. He led by example. Guys knew that if he could put on a uniform with us, he would.

"And another thing he did was take away an atmosphere where guys would blame others for their own shortcomings. He came in and took all that away. Players still do that today, but Red would have none of it. I think Red did a little research into who was really behind the (Gang of 12) rebellion, and their asses were gone. I know that a few guys who started that deal were not part of the team. He wanted to know who some of the unsavory guys were who blamed others except themselves."

## The First Game

Morton's first regular-season game with the Broncos came on September 7, 1977, at Mile High Stadium. If not for a great performance by Denver's defense, Morton could easily have been booed back to his car, just like in New York.

Morton went 12–20 passing, for 144 yards and one interception. But the Broncos won, 7–0, over the St. Louis Cardinals. The lone score came on a 10-yard touchdown run by Otis Armstrong.

What Morton most remembers about the game was the week leading up to it. The Cardinals arrived in Denver several days in advance to better acclimate themselves to the altitude. Miller knew right away that was a mistake.

"I remember Red saying, 'We've got 'em already.' He just thought that the Cardinals maybe had already psyched themselves out, that they were thinking of other things besides the football game. I guess, looking back, he was right. But it was an ugly win. It wasn't the kind of offensive performance I wanted to have in my first game as a Bronco, but we got the win. The defense showed right away what kind of defense they would become. They bailed us out that day…and did a few other times too."

## The First "Big" Bronco Win

Game 5, at Oakland, was the one many Broncomaniacs remember as establishing the team as an NFL powerhouse in 1977. The Broncos came to Alameda County Coliseum on October 16 with a 4–0 record. Big deal, critics said. The Broncos had only beaten some mediocre teams, including the second-year Seattle Seahawks. The world-champion Raiders and quarterback Ken Stabler would crush the so-called Orange Crush defense. Not quite.

Not only did the Broncos win, they humiliated the Raiders, 30–7. The Orange Crush picked off Stabler a record seven times. Denver spotted Oakland the game's first seven points, then dominated every second thereafter. One of the highlights was a fake field goal, which led to a 25-yard touchdown pass from holder Norris Weese to kicker Jim Turner.

Morton most recalls the feeling of jubilation in the locker room…and Stabler seeming to have no idea where he was throwing the ball all day.

"You heard a lot of stories about Stabler, and maybe you thought, 'Has he been out drinking all night?' or something. But he was a great competitor and I just think our defense had one of the all-time great games that day. To intercept a guy like Stabler that many times, I mean it was unheard of. But he didn't seem to give a damn where the ball was going. He just kept flinging it.

"I remember all of us thinking after the game, 'Hey, we're pretty damn good.' I don't think Oakland thought much of us. They looked down their noses at us. I remember the touchdown Turner scored a lot, too. We never thought he was going to get to the end zone. He wasn't the speediest guy to begin with, and to see those black high-top shoes of his pumping was pretty funny. I might have been the only guy on the team slower than him.

"That game really reinforced what I'd always believed to be true, because of how the defense played. That was our team's strength. But we were an opportunistic offensive team, too. A lot of our guys really started to believe after that game. I'd been through some great years in Dallas and been to a Super Bowl, but none of our other guys had experienced anything like we were starting to go through. Red Miller was going berserk, and so was our G.M., Fred Gehrke—a really great man.

"Everybody was just so excited. I remember looking at Louis Wright (who ran an interception back for a touchdown) and we both just kind of went, 'Damn.' I called him 'Boog-a-loo,' because he was always dancing all the time. And of course he was after the game. Of all our 12 wins in the regular season, that was the biggest, no question."

## Week 7—Payback

In 1977, by Week 7, Mile High Stadium truly was rocking. The Broncos were 6–0, and the Raiders were in town. Denver already had one rout against Oakland, and now they had home-field advantage. The usual orange-clad crowd of 76,000 packed the stadium and gave their heroes a massive ovation.

After three quarters, Mile High was dead silent. The Raiders showed why they were still world champions, jumping out to a 24–0 lead entering the fourth quarter before the Broncos scored the game's final 14 points. So much for the perfect season.

Morton threw for 242 yards in a losing cause, while Stabler only needed to throw 14 times, finishing with 70 yards. But Oakland played a great defensive game through the first three quarters.

"That was our first hiccup. Nothing went right. The Raiders, they came to play that day. They had some amazing Hall of Fame players on that team, and you could tell they were ready to play, after what we'd done to them. It was disappointing to lose that game, but they were a great team. They had field position on us all day. Even though we lost, and it wasn't fun, I think the fact that we scored the last 14 points of the game and had a real good fourth quarter made us come out of that game with still a good attitude, that we were still a real good team."

## Super Bowl Preview

A lot of people predicted a Super Bowl preview when the Broncos met the Dallas Cowboys in the last regular-season game of 1977. The 12–1 Broncos took on the 11–2 Cowboys at Texas Stadium, each having wrapped up the best records in their conference.

Craig Morton was not looking ahead to anything more than getting out of Dallas in one piece.

A couple weeks before, he suffered a hip-pointer injury—one of the most painful injuries for an athlete. Because of the pain, Morton didn't want to play in the game at Dallas. But coach Red Miller wanted to not only keep his soon-to-be playoff starting quarterback sharp, he wanted to throw off the Dallas defensive scheme by playing Morton at least one series. Miller, as always, wanted to win, even though this game meant nothing in the standings.

"Nobody wanted to let on that I was hurt. I had in my mind that I didn't want to play. But I also thought that maybe it would be good to play, to get a look at their defense, blitz-wise. The rest would have been good but Red and I talked it over and he said maybe I should just play a series. I said it was a great idea. Well, of course, in my one series, Cliff Harris and Charlie Waters—two of my best buddies from playing before in Dallas—blitzed me up the middle and popped it again. It started bleeding again. I just fell right on top of the hip again and said, 'Shoot.' I knew from that point on, for a few weeks, it wasn't going to be any fun."

Morton was in extreme pain the rest of the postseason, and unable to practice for one whole week before the AFC Championship Game against Oakland. The Cowboys won the game, 14–6, with Morton throwing only one pass.

## History Is Made: A Playoff Victory

It was the night before Christmas, and 76,000-plus creatures were stirring at Mile High Stadium.

The first playoff game in Denver Broncos history was definitely an event, with scalpers getting the unheard of sum of up to $35 for a good seat! The formidable Pittsburgh Steelers were coming to town. The Steelers roster included numerous players that would make the Pro Football Hall of Fame. Terry Bradshaw, Lynn Swann, John Stallworth, Mean Joe Greene, Jack Lambert—the list seemed endless.

Pundits predicted a Pittsburgh victory, even though the Broncos had beaten the Steelers handily in the regular season and had home-field advantage. In 1977, that was quite an edge. There simply was no louder crowd in the NFL that season, and it was certainly that way in this holiday atmosphere.

The only trouble was the Broncos were hurting. Morton's hip was killing him. He spent most of his days on the training table, not only receiving aid from the team medical staff, but from the aspiring chiropractor, teammate Jack Dolbin.

Dolbin really did work toward a degree in the relatively new medical science, and Morton credits him for much of his being able to play that week and the next. Dolbin converted a room in his Arvada house to a treatment area, and Morton would drive over and get fixed up by the Doc.

*For years, no one knew that Morton spent the week leading up to the AFC Championship game in a hospital with a swollen hip and leg, barely able to walk. A series of big passes to Moses Haven led the Broncos to their first AFC title over the Oakland Raiders, and a trip to Super Bowl XII.* Photo courtesy of WireImages.

The team's best defensive player, Randy Gradishar, also was limping around with a sprained ankle.

Orange Crush mania was in full bloom. Newspapers from around the country started to really take note that several houses in Denver had the curious color scheme of orange with blue trim. In Terry Frei's book, *77: Denver, the Broncos and a Coming of Age*, former Denver sportscaster Ron Zappolo remembered the week well.

"Every night we're doing stories on guys who paint their houses orange, people who paint their toilets orange," Zappolo recalls. "I wish I could say I'm making this stuff up. I'm not! … People sent me the most amazing crap every week. The pictures! People would take pictures of them painting themselves orange and told me, 'Put this on the air.' I gave it away to people at Ch. 4 because we didn't have room for it. Orange gloves, orange napkin holders, orange this, orange that.'"

The decibel level, although never officially recorded in the game, might have easily surpassed 120 at times. Morton had

*The 3-4 defense of the Broncos, known as the Orange Crush, had the NFL's number-one defense against the rush in 1977.* Photo courtesy of AP Images.

always trained himself not to hear a thing on the field, other than the machinations and conclusions of his own mind. However, he heard the opening introductions.

"It was just one of the most festive atmospheres I ever remember for a football game. It's the day before Christmas and there's a playoff game in Denver—the first in team history. I couldn't help but get some goose bumps, and I almost never got them. I always had my mind focused squarely on the game and nothing at all about the crowd or the conditions."

The game was a thriller. The Steelers played well, drawing even in the fourth quarter, 21–21. The Steelers, Super Bowl champions two years before, had a swagger that hadn't gone away—particularly on defense—led by Mean Joe Greene.

"He would always just be on the line, in his crouch, looking up and smiling at me," Morton said. "He would just laugh and say, 'I'm gonna getcha, Craig. I'm gonna getcha.'"

But Greene would have no chance to get at Morton that day when, during the game, he was ejected for punching Broncos guard Paul Howard in the stomach. It was an inconceivable loss of composure by Greene, and it helped the Broncos. The Broncos would win their first playoff game, 34–21. Two Jim Turner field goals got them to a 27–21 lead, then Morton salted the game away with a 34-yard touchdown pass to Doc Dolbin.

Dolbin beat Steelers backup secondary man, Jimmy Allen, on his route. Otherwise, Dolbin would have had to go against the great Mel Blount, and things no doubt would have been tougher.

"I came up to the line and called an audible. Then I called timeout and said, 'Coach, we got 'em. I knew what we were going to do, and we were going to get a touchdown.' But everybody said, 'no no, we don't want to do that.' And I said, 'No, we're going to do this.' And they said, 'no.' And we were still arguing as I was running back on the field. Well, the play comes in from the sidelines and I say, 'Bullshit. Jack, you're scoring.' So I just called the play, and they actually played a different defense than I thought! But Jack made a good move and I just hit him, and it put the game away. It was a madhouse at the end of the game. I had never heard fans so loud."

After the win, with fans going delirious, Broncos coach Miller had some cross words with Steelers coaches, over the Greene punch on Howard. Earlier in the season, Greene had hit Howard with another cheap shot in the groin.

The Broncos had their usual victory party at the Colorado Mine Company, with players drinking out of a massive punch bowl filled with fruit juice, soda, and vodka. Morton was feeling no pain until the next day, when he realized his hip was killing him again.

## "It Looked Like He'd Been Hit By a Car"

When looking at the final statistics of the 1978 AFC Championship Game it would seem just like another typical Bronco victory of that special season. And, in many ways, it was.

But there was absolutely nothing normal about the condition in which Craig Morton played. His painful left hip had gotten worse after the victory over the Steelers.

It was not revealed at the time, but the truth is Morton never practiced in the week leading up to the showdown with the hated, world champion Oakland Raiders. Now, his entire left leg had swollen, filled with what he said were two inches around of blood. This would be the most important week of practice in the season, but it was soon clear to coach Miller that his starting quarterback would not be able to partake.

Still, the media and public at large never found out until years later that Morton spent his days at St. Luke's Medical Center in Denver. In today's 24/7 media world, keeping secret that a starting quarterback wasn't at practice entering a championship game would be virtually impossible. But with practices closed to the media, and everybody keeping a poker face in the locker room to the press on hand, somehow it never got out that Morton was an invalid that week. Only on the Friday before the game did Miller acknowledge that Morton hadn't been practicing, but still kept quiet the extent of Morton's injury. To all Coloradoans, there was little question No. 7 would be in the lineup against the Al Davis's "Raidahs."

"The leg was black, really. I was like, 'I'm dying, I've got to go to the hospital.' I had a nice private room. I really couldn't get out of bed. But nobody knew. I was just always getting treatment, not really talking to anybody. Guys like Dolbin would come in and visit me, though, and help give treatments. He had heard of this machine that he thought could help, which moved the blood around a little bit or something. Hell, I tried anything. But really it was horrible and wasn't getting any better."

Morton resigned himself to the situation the night before. With the Raiders installed in Las Vegas as 3½-point favorites, he was going to miss the game that, if won, would put the Broncos into the Super Bowl.

Still, he came to Mile High Stadium in the morning to take more treatment and just support his teammates. He spent a long time in the whirlpool

"So I got up on a training table, so everyone could see me. The leg was absolutely black. I thought, 'Well, I'll get a little sympathy here.' But after a little while, I started to think more about giving it a shot."

That's when one of the most memorable stories of Broncos lore happened. Miller kept coming around Morton's locker every few minutes as game time neared, asking him what he thought. Morton had decided to put his uniform on, and had no trouble getting his shirt and upper pad on. But anything involving his legs was a chore, especially getting on his shoes. Doing that by himself, in fact, was out of the question.

Morton then memorably told Miller, "Okay, if you can tie my shoes, I'll try it."

"But, really, I was just kind of saying it in a joking way. Really, I was still not sure I could walk out on the field. But when he got down on his hands and knees and tied my shoes, he did it in front of everybody. And after he did that, I got a little fired up and said, 'I'm ready.'

Morton's teammates got fired up just seeing him give it a go.

Said kicker Jim Turner, "Honestly, it looked like Craig had been hit by a car. His leg looked really very scary. He probably still should have been in a hospital. But this was the AFC title game. It's a testament to Craig's toughness that he did what he did."

Morton told Miller he'd start the game and see how it went, knowing that one big hit on his left leg would probably end his day or season.

"And just like I had hoped, as soon as I got on the field and the crowd started going crazy and I started throwing a football a little, adrenaline took over and I started not to feel it as much. And when I started taking some snaps and throwing, I found that I could set up good, but any time I started to move forward, it still really hurt. And I just told my linemen: 'Guys, they don't touch me, we win this game.' And they did an unreal job. They only hit me twice, and I fell on the other side each time. And to do that against that defensive line, with the players they had, was some kind of accomplishment."

The game was another thriller. It still ranks as the favorite victory in Broncos history to some fans, given that it put the team into its first Super Bowl. With their one-legged quarterback, the Broncos dethroned the champion Raiders, 20–17.

Morton's start was not encouraging, however. His first pass went right between the numbers of Raiders Pro Bowler, Jack Tatum. Fortunately, Tatum dropped the easy interception.

The Raiders took a 3–0 lead on an Errol Mann field goal, but Morton found his favorite receiver, Haven Moses, across the middle for what ended up a 74-yard, first-quarter touchdown. Despite the close final score, the Broncos would never trail from that point.

Morton recalls the big strike to Moses—and the near-interception by Tatum:

"On the first pass, we called a '143 Dig', one of our favorite plays. It was Haven across the middle. But I threw it right into Tatum's chest. So after that I said we weren't going to throw over the middle anymore. I wanted to fake over the middle and go to Haven in the corner. We did that. I got some good zip on the pass and he caught it, and I just remember thinking how incredible it was that he kept going down the sidelines.

"I hit Haven with another (12-yard touchdown) pass in the fourth quarter, that made it 20–10, and at that point I really couldn't hear myself think from the crowd noise. I don't think a crowd was ever so loud, honest to God.

The Raiders scored late on a Ken Stabler-to-Dave Casper touchdown pass and there were some tense moments in the end, but when the gun sounded the Broncos were AFC Champions. They were going to the Super Bowl!

Morton finished the most gutsy game of his career 10-for-20 passing, with 224 yards, the two touchdown strikes to Moses and one interception. Morton was overcome with emotion in the shower afterward, water coming from his eyes as well as the nozzles.

"Somebody snapped that picture, I remember seeing it, and it was something I'll never forget obviously. Other than my kids being born, that was probably the greatest feeling I ever had in my life. I had been to a Super Bowl before with Dallas, but for some reason, this was better. These people in Denver were the reason. They were just amazing. This just wasn't supposed to happen in Denver. They were a Cow Town. It just seemed to change everything about the city.

"I remember just standing in the doorway, from the South Stands. I couldn't move too well, obviously, so I just was standing there and it was beyond anything I could imagine. Everybody was just going crazy. We went to the Colorado Mine Company after the game, of course, and I made sure I kept feeling no pain. We had a few vodka and orange juices, that's for sure. They had the best steaks there, and the food never tasted so good as that night. It's so amazing to think back to that day, because of how it started out for me, and how it turned out at the end. I went from thinking seriously I wouldn't be able to play to sipping champagne and winning an AFC Championship. I had an incredible amount of help from a great bunch of teammates that day. It was a great team victory, one that I'll never forget."

## Roger Staubach: Words from a friend

Craig Morton had so many teammates in the NFL, it could take 10 books to chronicle all the things they might say about him. But one teammate in particular has meant a lot to him over the years: Cowboys legendary QB Roger Staubach.

They were teammates for five years in Dallas, but also rivals. They played against each other in college, including in an all-star game, then vied for the starting QB job with the Cowboys from 1969 to 1973, then competed for a Super Bowl title in 1978.

It would be normal for some hard feelings to develop with all that competition, but they never did. Thirty years after beating Morton in Super Bowl XII, Staubach has maintained a good friendship with him. Because of Morton's inner makeup, that is easy to do, Staubach said.

"Craig was always somebody that everyone feels good about," Staubach said. "He's a good person. Of course, I followed the Cowboys for four years when I was still in the Navy (after being drafted in 1964 by Dallas) and followed what was going on between Don Meredith and Craig. The year I retired from the Navy, Meredith retired that same summer. So then it was Craig and I. At first, coach Landry kept me as Craig's backup and got along with him very well. He was always nice to me out on the field. I probably would have ended up someplace else if he didn't have all the injuries he did. I think the worst one he had was in Atlanta, in the '69 season. He had gotten off to a great start, and he got hit by Tommy Nobis, and they both got hurt on the same play. Craig got a separated shoulder, and Nobis hurt his knee. He played the rest of the year, but that shoulder was definitely bothering him."

Staubach and Morton not only alternated starts at times during their time together, they even alternated plays. At one point in the 1971 season, Landry sent Staubach and Morton in and out for successive plays in a game against the Chicago Bears, a 23-19 Bears win. Staubach assumed the starting role the next week and led Dallas on a 10-game win streak that culminated with a 24–3 victory over Miami in Super Bowl VI. Staubach missed most of the

*Cowboys legendary quarterback Roger Staubach and Morton were once teammates, then rivals, then Super Bowl adversaries, but always remained friends.* Photo courtesy of WireImages.

following season with a separated shoulder, and Morton did a fine job in relief. But Staubach relieved Morton in a playoff game against San Francisco, led Dallas to a come-from-behind win, and never relinquished the starting job again.

"But there was never really any controversy, and certainly never between him and me," Staubach said. "We alternated as starting quarterbacks to start the '71 season. Craig started the first game, and we won, and then I started the second week, against the Eagles, and got knocked out in the first quarter. Craig came in and we killed the Eagles, so the next week, he started, and it wasn't looking good for me there. So, he started the next week, but we lost to the Redskins. So then we went back to this kind of alternating system. That game against the Bears, coach Landry announced before the game we'd be alternating plays. Craig and I looked at each other, and just kind of shook our heads. We couldn't believe it. But we just did it, and got along fine still."

"Craig was just always first class about how he treated me—and I was the guy trying to take his job. I was 29 by the time I got a chance to start [because of his Naval commitments]. Craig and I never had a problem, but I think the team was kind of divided. Probably a lot of the team wanted Craig, and a lot of the team wanted me. I understand why Craig wanted a trade by the time he went to the Giants, though. He was too good a quarterback to not be playing with someone. The year before we traded him, I played pretty much the whole season [1973] and he was still the perfect teammate. He was the backup quarterback all year, but was still a first-class guy. He could have pouted, but he was always there trying to help me."

When Staubach's Cowboys beat Morton's Broncos in Super Bowl XII, Staubach was the first person to shake Morton's hand in consolation. There certainly wouldn't be any gloating from Roger the Dodger toward his former teammate.

"That particular game, we got the breaks," Staubach said. "After the first quarter, our defense just played unbelievable. If I was on Denver's team, the score would have been the same as it turned out. You could have had God back there playing QB, and our defense would have gotten Him. Craig didn't really get much of a chance. Our offense did fine, and had a couple of big plays, but it was really our defense that won that game. Denver played so well that year, and Craig had such a great year for them and in the playoffs."

When Morton went through his financial problems after his career, Staubach lent a helping hand, some through specific financial counsel, but mostly just the emotional support of a friend.

"I think the world of Craig, and he was probably taken advantage of by some people," Staubach said. "He cares about people, and some people took advantage of that. But he's admitted that, you know, you make those decisions at times. But at the end of the day, if you talk to anybody that knows Craig, they think the world of him."

## Loren Hawley: The Enabler

Loren Hawley's life is so full of stories and intrigue, it's worth a book in itself. In fact, much of his life was detailed in Larry Colton's 1993 book, *Goat Brothers.*

Who is Loren Hawley? He is probably Craig Morton's best friend, a legendary rugby player at Cal-Berkeley, who was a receiver on a couple of Morton's Cal football teams. Hawley later went into business with Morton on several ventures that had many ups and downs.

Hawley, a fun-loving, hard-living, self-described country bumpkin, became so entwined with Morton that he lived wherever Morton played much of his career. He was living in Denver, therefore, on the day of the 1977 AFC Championship Game against the Oakland Raiders, when Morton was hospitalized much of the week because of a badly bruised left leg and hip.

What has been underreported, however, is the role Hawley played in Morton's eventual decision to play. Basically, it came down to Hawley telling his friend, "Get out there and play the damn game! You've worked too hard for this moment, now get your ass out of bed."

The common legend of the game is that Red Miller was the one who most prodded Morton into playing, by eagerly tying his shoelaces after Morton asked for help. But it was really words from Hawley's mouth that had the biggest influence. Working in the Denver oil business at the time and living with Morton, Hawley visited the hospital the morning of the game to see his good buddy.

"I was ready to just say, 'Hell, this has been a great year. I got them to the championship, but I'm hurting. There is nothing I can think that is going to be fun getting out of bed and playing in this game.' But then Loren just looked at me like I had done many times with him and said, 'What are you talking about?' You can't afford not to play in this game. You've worked all your life to get back to this situation. Get your ass up. I'll take you over there. Let's go.'

"And that's exactly what happened. And the thing is, he was right. That helped me learn right there that you can always do things you don't think you can, if you really want to. I didn't think I could do it. But once he started talking in the positive sense, that it was something that was GOING to happen, it started a different thought process entirely. He took away any possibility that I would not play. So, when that happened, I just said, 'Okay, I'm going to do this.' And then once I got around my teammates and got in the locker room, I just kept getting more and more inspired."

Today, Hawley can't speak because of cancer, but remains Morton's closest confidante and an inspiration.

"He's just a great man, a real character guy, and a great f*ck-up! And, believe me, a woman magnet. He was a great, great athlete who finally just got elected to the Cal Hall of Fame—which was long overdue. Without him that day, though, I seriously doubt I would have played against the Raiders."

Sadly, Loren died on April 6, 2008.


## Super Bowl XII—Disaster In New Orleans

When Craig Morton is asked to think back to Super Bowl XII at the Louisiana Superdome, his naturally cordial tone gets somber and grim. And not just because of the final score: Dallas Cowboys 27, Denver Broncos 10. Bring up New Orleans 1978 to many Bronco players, and the first thing they'll tell you about is nothing from the game. It was the dump of a hotel the NFL gave them.

"We had the worst accommodations. It still makes me mad thinking about that hotel. It was horrible. There were cockroaches everywhere, the walls were paper-thin. It was dark and depressing and just terrible. The Cowboys were staying at the same facility

*Despite the frenzy of "Broncomania" in Denver, the energy did not transfer to New Orleans, where Broncos lost Super Bowl XII to the Cowboys, 27–10.* Photo courtesy of AP Images.

they had when I played in the Super Bowl with them in '71. Those were much better. But we were right by the airport in this dump. When some of the wives came in at midnight or whatever, after being out on the town, you could hear them screaming and they'd wake you up. The accommodations were so horrible that it really started to dig at people. It really pissed everybody off to be treated so badly… Then there was the practice facility; we practiced at the old Tulane Stadium. It was muddy; there were no other facilities. Most of the time, we had to come back to the hotel to shower. It was like being in grammar school."

Compounding Morton's problems was his still-painful left side, which was improving but would not be 100 percent by game time. There also was a report from the IRS that stated Morton had some problems. The Tax Man had placed a $34,000 lien against him, and the story was reported to the wire services then picked up by many major newspapers. Morton continues to call the story "bullshit—I paid my taxes," but had to deal with the distraction of being asked about it in the week before the game.

But it wasn't all bad in New Orleans. Morton did enjoy riding the wave of excitement to Super Bowl XII.

"A lot of my friends from Dallas and New York came to New Orleans and they gave me a nice dinner down on Bourbon Street. And the week before, back in Denver, was great. We had a kind of spur-of-the-moment parade, which was great. We were focusing on the Cowboys, but everywhere we went we were being mobbed and Denver was just off its rocker by then with hype and fun and just craziness about the Broncos."

Bronco fans were at their giddiest with Orange Crush fever. After the Broncos beat the Raiders, 65,000 Orange Crush T-shirts were sold in about two days. A local retail outlet, Fred Schmid, had Orange Tag sales in place of the usual red. In a big orange ad, a department store called "The Denver" proclaimed: "Go ahead and try to ride 'em, Cowboys…you'll find our Broncos can't be busted." It was impossible to get through to a travel agent to try and book a trip to New Orleans. In his book, *Orange Madness*, longtime Denver sports columnist Woody Paige gave the following description of some of the symptoms of Orange Crush Fever:

- Stiffness of the index finger—caused by repeatedly signaling No. 1
- Compulsion to purchase anything orange—it was estimated that 50 new items were going on sale weekly
- Sprained knee joints—caused by constant jumping up and down at Broncos games.

Super Bowl XII jumpstarted a new era in the way the event was covered, and how it eventually became America's biggest sports day and one of the biggest events commercially. CBS Television got a record $344,000 for one-minute commercials. It was also the first Super Bowl to be played indoors, and broadcasters soon found that the games came across better in that environment, because of more enhanced and enclosed sound. The Cowboys, 12–2 in the regular season, were installed as five-point favorites by the Vegas wise guys. Morton and the Broncos had their work cut out for them.

"I knew it was going to be a tough game against Dallas. They were just probably the one team in the NFL that we didn't match up well against. Their front-four defensive line was just something that was really hard for us to go up against. I was still hurting a lot, too. I mean, it was good to have that first week off, but I was still not good.

"I wasn't the only player not doing great physically. Randy Gradishar had a bad ankle that had been giving him problems for a couple of weeks; and I'll never forget—under one of the stands of the Sugar Bowl (Tulane Stadium) that was half torn down, because they were in the process of tearing it down, Red Miller called everybody together and wanted to have a weigh-in. One of our key players was Tom Glassic, a guard on our offensive line. He had been sick that week, and he gets on the scale and he weighs like 226 pounds are something. And I said to myself, 'We are screwed.' He had to go up against Randy White (*author's note: who, ironically, was the draft pick Dallas took in exchange for trading Morton to the Giants*). I knew there was no way he could block that guy, he had lost too much weight. I went back and started to try and figure some other way we could block him. It was just very unfortunate. Mentally, it did not do anybody any good on our offense to know that Glassic was only weighing in the 220s and had to go against a future Hall of Famer."

When people today look at the final score, they think it was a blowout. But it could have been different by a few bounces of the football. On the Cowboys' first possession, a double reverse, receiver Butch Johnson fumbled a pass completion from Roger Staubach. But Johnson recovered on the Cowboys' 20. On Denver's first possession, Morton drove his team to the Dallas 33, but took an 11-yard sack on third down and Bucky Dilts punted the ball to the Dallas 1-yard line and receiver Tony Hill dropped the ball. With Broncos special teams men beating down on Hill, he recovered and stayed out of the end zone. Unbelievably, on their ensuing series, the Cowboys fumbled again, but Cowboys center John Fitzgerald recovered Tony Dorsett's drop. The Broncos' defense got the ball back to Morton in a scoreless game, but when the Denver offense made a miscue with the football for the

*Broncos head coach Red Miller congratulates Dallas' Tom Landry after Cowboys win Super Bowl XII. Sick players, numerous turnovers, and interceptions plagued the Broncos throughout the game, resulting in a 27–10 loss.* Photo courtesy of AP Images.

first time, Dallas recovered. Morton, under heavy pressure all day from co-Most Valuable Players White and Harvey Martin, threw a hurried pass that was intercepted by Dallas' Randy Hughes on the Denver 25. Five plays later, Dorsett was in the end zone for a 7–0 lead. On the next series, Morton was intercepted again, by Aaron Kyle. The turnover was turned into an Efren Herrera field goal.

Denver's Billy Thompson intercepted Staubach in the end zone in the second quarter, but the referees ruled Staubach had his foot out of bounds when he threw the ball. Replays showed Staubach's foot clearly was in, but the call stood and Dallas ended up getting a field goal again, for a 13–0 lead.

That's the way it went all day for the Broncos. Unlike anytime in the regular season, they were beating themselves, with turnovers and the inability to capitalize on others' mistakes. Morton, who finished the day 4–15 passing with four interceptions, was lifted from the game in the third quarter in favor of Norris Weese. Weese helped lead a drive that led to a Rob Lytle touchdown run that cut the Dallas lead to 20–10, but the game was lost for good when fullback Robert Newhouse threw an option touchdown pass to Golden Richards.

Thirty years later, Super Bowl XII is still tough for Morton to think about.

"We couldn't take advantage of anything, and I had a horrible game. They really were getting a rush on me, and we had no running game and were forced to pass. And you can't pass against that rush, because they killed people. Realistically, yes, we probably were a team that was a little too inexperienced and 'happy to be there' for that game, at least more than Dallas. But with our defense, we just felt we could go in there and play like we had all year and win, and we didn't. The offense turned the ball over too much. We just could never get in the game. We had no different game plan against them than any other team. It was just 'take what they give you, play for field position, and take advantage of some breaks.' And we got some breaks, but we just could not get that last favorable bounce. That punt fumble by Hill that we didn't recover—if we do, we're up 7–0 and maybe the game shifts in a whole new direction after that. But they got it instead. We needed some turnover to get into the game so we could play our game. But because we got behind, we were forced to play catchup and that wasn't our game.

"I had some things that I thought I could take advantage of with that Dallas defense that day, and they figured that that's what I'd be looking for, and they changed up. I thought I could get some good reads off D.D. Lewis, their weak-side linebacker. All the film I was watching, he was always doing the same thing. And then he changed up completely for the Super Bowl game, (for) which I have to give him a lot of credit. I didn't think he'd ever think about doing that.

"We also went up against a great coach, in Tom Landry. Of course, I played for him for many years. He just walked his walk and he never varied. He was a great teacher and knew more about football than any person I've ever known. He knew about all aspects of the game. He was quiet, but tough, and you knew he

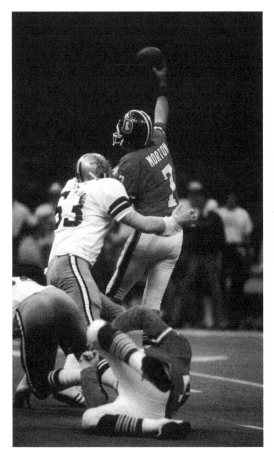

*Craig Morton (7) throws a pass against Cowboys offense but cannot generate enough to win Super Bowl XII in New Orleans.*

carried the big stick. He was sort of like my dad, where you knew you better not screw up. He obviously had a good game plan, which was probably: get to the quarterback and kick the shit out of him. That usually works."

"The thing about losing in the Super Bowl is this: you go from being at the highest of highs as a football player two weeks before to not being able to get any lower. I remember, after the game, we'd had a big post-game party planned. John Denver was there, and it was all supposed to be so great and it was just so bad. After a while, I was so depressed that I just got up and went out to Bourbon Street with a friend. Nobody was out at all. It was like a ghost town. Me and my buddy Loren Hawley ran into Jerry Jeff

Walker, the country-western singer. So, we just walked around with him and had a few cocktails together that night.

"One of the things I remember about that game is looking up at the Superdome ceiling, because I was on my back so much. I could count the tiles on the ceiling. But I still beat myself up over that game. It'll never go away. I'm very proud that we were the first Denver Broncos team to go to the Super Bowl, and we really did change Denver. But of all the days of my career, that was the worst. I would still choose to go to the Super Bowl every time, because it's a great experience and you have to do so many great things to get there. But, as I said before, it wasn't just the game that left so many horrible memories. It was that damn hotel."

*"The thing about losing in the Super Bowl is that you go from being at the highest of highs… to not being able to get any lower,"* says Broncos quarterback, Craig Morton. The Broncos lost to the Dallas Cowboys 27–10 at Super Bowl XII. Photo courtesy of AP Images.

Woody Paige wrote one of the more memorable opening sentences in Denver sports writing history after Super Bowl XII. Morton had recently become a born-again Christian.

"Craig Morton found Jesus, but couldn't find Moses," Paige wrote in the *Rocky Mountain News*, referencing Haven Moses, who was open on one key passing play but was underthrown, leading to a costly interception by Benny Barnes.

"I've never watched a tape of that game, and never will. I still think about the game sometimes late at night. It's not pleasant at all, but it doesn't go away. I never look at the [AFC Championship] ring we got. It's packed away somewhere. People were great to me after…the fans, which was great. And they continue to be so about that game to me. But obviously, Super Bowl XII is not my favorite subject."

Cowboys assistant coach Dan Reeves, Morton's great friend, recalls the lucky feeling his team had entering the day.

"We knew Craig was hurt," Reeves said. "He played with amazing guts against the Raiders, but you could tell he was still hurting by the time of that game. It was just a good day for us, but of course in the joy of winning, you knew Craig was hurting afterward, not just physically. So, that took a little bit of the joy out of it for me at least. But he wouldn't want any sympathy from anybody, so I won't start that now. We just had a very good day defensively and got a few breaks along the way. It was just our day."

# chapter 2
# The Last Denver Years

*"I should have caught the pass. It hit my hands. But we shouldn't have been throwing the football in that situation…. We learned a lesson."*

—Dan Reeves

Craig Morton would never play in a Super Bowl again, but it wasn't for a lack of trying. The man who was supposed to have been all washed up played another four years, and he never had a losing record as a starting quarterback in Denver.

## 1978

The follow-up season to the Broncos' first Super Bowl appearance, on the surface, went well. But the reality is there was plenty of turmoil—some of it predictable. The Kumbaya-singing, Cinderella team of the year before can easily turn into a sniping and fractured one the next when players want to cash in and feel they aren't being appreciated.

That's basically what happened with the '78 Broncos, although they still managed a solid 10–6 record and another playoff berth.

Morton doesn't remember the season with particular fondness. A rift developed between Morton and coach Red Miller. Morton believes Miller lost a lot of faith him in him after the Super Bowl, and started to change in unexpected ways toward his team. In a nutshell, Morton suggests that perhaps Miller needed a bigger hat size.

"I knew the minute we got to training camp that things were kind of changing a little bit. Not only had we just lost the thing that we all wanted, but I just kind of felt with Red that everybody was at fault and he was kind of above it all. And that's really hard for me to say, because I love Red Miller. But he just had an attitude that he was Mr. Miller now, not the same Red we knew. Maybe I'm just being a little paranoid, I don't know. But I just felt that he was always thinking, 'Geez, if I just had a quarterback that could finish it out, then we could win the big game.'

"I think he changed for everybody a little bit. Because, the blame went to everybody that lost the Super Bowl, and he was the only guy that didn't get any. That's kind of how it came off to the players. He and I had some real heated discussions that year. I was the team captain and he'd say, 'How the hell can you be team captain?' and I'd tell him 'I don't know what happened to you, but come on, this team used to LOVE you.' He was coach of the year and I was player of the year in '77, and I think that he thought he was more coach of the year than I was player of the year. But it's all a bunch of crap, individual awards, because it's the team that does it. Neither of us could have won anything without the team. I mean, I was a piece of crap in New York the year before and the next year I'm player of the year?

"He just started to be different with me. He started benching me, but then he'd come to me and say, 'Hey, you gotta get us out of this jam.' So, some resentment started building up in me. I'd kind of start thinking, 'Oh sure, *now* you need me' in those moments, which might have been a little selfish on my part, and I'm not saying I was a saint with Red either. But some friction started to develop, there's no question."

Friction started to really develop after the Broncos lost a 31–28 game at Mile High Stadium to the New York Jets, on

*After the loss in Super Bowl XII, coach Red Miller focused his energies on new prospects, possibly driving a rift between existing players.* Photo courtesy of AP Images.

November 5. The Jets had a young quarterback out of Georgia, Matt Robinson, who Miller became enamored with after his performance. Miller, Morton said, openly coveted Robinson and the Broncos would trade a first- and second-round draft choice, plus Craig Penrose, to land him in 1980. Robinson started seven games that season, and was a total bust; he threw only two touchdown passes and a whopping 12 interceptions, forcing Miller to still reluctantly call on the old pro—Morton.

"Red just needed Robinson. That was just his deal. He was going to be 'the guy.' But Matt just didn't have it. I mean, he was a good quarterback, but he was very spindly and he just couldn't withstand the rigors of a season, without some help. So, I would still be around, just trying to do what I always did. But it's harder when you don't know if you're going to be playing that day.

"I just wasn't Red's guy anymore after that Super Bowl. I remember talking with Babe Parilli one day the next year, and Babe and I were as close as any two people could be. He was my quarterbacks coach, and I just remember him telling me basically, 'Look, you're just on Red's shit list.' Again, maybe I just misread the situation. Because I was the starter going into the '78 season and I still started most of the games. But I just know that at some point in that year, he started trying to get me out of the lineup. That's okay. That's professional sports and I was a big boy. But I guess you could say the honeymoon was over between me and Red not too long after that Super Bowl, although I always respected him as a coach and a man. You don't always get along with your boss, and that's normal. So, I don't look back with a lot of bitterness at that time. But that's just the fact of the matter, that there was some turbulence starting with that year."

Still, the Broncos were a winning team. The season started on a great note, a 14–6 win over the Raiders at Mile High Stadium, in which Morton threw for 201 yards. The Orange Crush defense was still that, finishing second in the NFL in fewest points allowed. The league expanded the schedule that year to 16 games, and Morton started 13 of them, completing 54.7 percent of his passes, with 11 touchdowns and eight interceptions. But the

*After their Super Bowl defeat, the Broncos came back to a strong record, with the Orange Crush defense still second in the NFL in fewest points allowed. A few changes included an extended playing schedule and Craig Morton (l) and Matt Robinson alternated starting quarterback position for the 1980 season.*

Broncos badly lacked a top running back. The leading rusher was Lonnie Perrin, with 455 yards—still a modern-era low for a team in a 16-game season. Rob Lytle, so important in the '77 Super Bowl run, was banged up most of the year and carried the ball only 81 times. Otis Armstrong was not the same runner anymore, and the Broncos were shut out in one game by San Diego, and lost a dismal 7–6 game to the Baltimore Colts in Week 8. But Morton still had a strong connection with receiver Haven Moses, and tight end Riley Odoms had a great year with 54 catches and a team-leading six touchdown receptions.

"We still had a really close-knit team. To this day, those Broncos teams, including the '78 team, were the closest I ever played on."

## Not According To The Plan

When the Broncos played the Steelers in a 1978 rematch of their playoff meeting the year before, they were sure they had a big edge on the vaunted Steel Curtain defense.

Broncos coaches had noticed on film that Steelers linebacker Andy Russell tipped off many plays and formations by how his foot was positioned. Morton went into the December 30 game at Three Rivers Stadium thinking he would exploit Russell all day.

It didn't exactly turn out that way.

Despite getting a quick 3–0 lead on a 37-yard Jim Turner field goal, the Steelers scored 33 of the game's final 40 points, for a 33–10 win. Like he did some of the regular season, Broncos coach Red Miller yanked Morton from the game early, replacing him with Norris Weese. Morton's final stats read: 3–5 passing for 34 yards, and he never could make out what Russell was doing.

"All we were paying attention to was his foot. We had noticed they would always run a certain defense if he had his left heel two inches off the ground. If he didn't, it would only be an inch, and a different scheme would be coming. Well, we had prepared for this, with all these audible systems. I would practice by looking over at the scout team and say, 'Get your heel up, then I'd call the play and it always worked.' Well, we got into the actual game and I couldn't see his foot well enough, whether it was one inch or two inches. I had no clue what he was doing. And I finally just yelled out to him, 'Would you get your heel up the way it's supposed to be up, because I can't call these plays. And we got killed, because we relied on this stupid ass scouting. We were wrong 100 percent of the time."

## Morton Shows 'em

John Elway is the Broncos quarterback most associated with great comeback victories, and rightfully so. But the best of all might belong to Morton. And, it was a game he didn't even play in the first half.

In 1979, former backup Norris Weese started six games. One of them was a September 23 game at Seattle, and the Seahawks looked to be on their way to an easy victory. Weese couldn't get much going, and Seattle was up big when Miller summoned Morton on the sidelines.

"He'd get himself into jams, then say, 'Craig, come here, come get us out of this.'

"Well, I had been trying to get myself mentally into the game even though I wasn't playing, and I was telling everybody that Seattle was playing this defense where you could do some 'turn-ins' and some 'gos' and do some fake routes and hit 'em deep. But nobody was listening to me, so I just said screw it, and went to go sit on my helmet.

"We were getting further and further behind, to where it was finally 34–10. So Red comes up to me and said, 'Craig, I want you to go in.' I said, 'you've got to be kidding! It's 34–10. I'll get killed! He said, 'I want you to go in' and I said I'm not going in. So, finally Haven (Moses) and a bunch of guys came over and said 'let's go.' I said, 'this is a joke,' but they kept at me and I said okay, I'll go.

"So, we get the ball and I go running out on the field and Red is just screaming at me, telling me 'This is the play I want you to run.' I said, 'You've got to be shitting me? You haven't listened to me all day and you want me to call this piece of shit play?' So I went in the huddle and said, 'Can you believe it, it's 34–10 and they still want to run a middle trap?' So, I said, 'Here's what we've got to do: Uppy [Rick Upchurch], you've got to make something happen immediately. So, we're just going to run a quick screen and you've got to get at least 10–15 yards, and get something happening.' So, we ran that play and we beat 'em 37–34. Upchurch started it, and Haven made some unbelievable plays, the defense started coming back and all of a sudden we've won the football game.

The greatest part of that game was our last touchdown, when Rob Lytle ran it in, and he immediately ran over to our sports information director, a guy named Bob Peck. Bob was dying of cancer, and he was sitting in a special chair. He'd lost all his hair from chemotherapy, was just sitting there, and Rob ran over to Bob and gave him the ball. To me, that's still one of the great moments in my career."

What was Miller like toward Morton after bailing his team out?

"Nothing. He probably said some good things about me to the press, but to me? Nothing."

## "Mister" Morton's Chair

Craig Morton never understood why any of his teammates stood up on the sidelines. It was hard enough on one's body being on the football field, why would anybody want to stand up and subject it to more strain when there was always the cushion of a football helmet to sit on? Morton stubbornly resisted calls to stop it, and took things a step further. He got a director's chair specially made for him. He used it at practices and, occasionally, at games, sitting at the north end of Mile High Stadium at the end of the bench.

"I used to get all kinds of shit for the helmet thing. So, I went out and had a director's chair made that said, "Mr. Morton" on the back. I had it put at the end of the bench, and whenever fans would give me shit, I would just go and sit in my chair. I would think, 'well how appreciative can you guys *not* be, so screw you. I'll go sit in my own director's chair.'

Some of the press wrote that I was an enigma on the team, that I was aloof from my teammates. But I was not aloof from them. I would always try to make all the time in the world for a teammate. I had all the respect in the world for them. But I'll admit I never liked getting benched, so when I wasn't playing, it was time to relax a little!"

## New Coach...At the Checkout Aisle

Times have certainly changed when it comes to communication. Today, it's impossible not to have news thrust at you 24 hours a day.

But when the Broncos made a coaching change in 1981, hiring Dan Reeves and firing Red Miller, Morton found out not from a text message or cell phone call. Instead, he heard it from a supermarket loudspeaker.

"Honest to God, I was shopping, I think at an Albertson's in Denver, when over the loudspeakers comes, 'Ladies and Gentlemen, we'd just like to inform you that the Denver Broncos have just hired Dan Reeves as their new coach."

"Well, I put my basket down and ran to a pay phone, to call Danny Reeves. Here's a guy I had played with as a teammate and also when he was a coach in Dallas. I got him and said, 'Unbelievable. I guess I can't call you 'Frog' anymore—that was his nickname. I said, 'I guess those days are gone now' and he said 'You're damned right they are.' He is a great person and a great coach."

Reeves recalls the phone call, and said he is grateful to have had his old friend as a quarterback in his first year as an NFL head coach.

"I never once had to worry about that position that year," Reeves said. "Obviously, the quarterback is an important position, and usually it's a learning process for player and coach in their first year together. But with Craig, I obviously had known him a long time, and I knew he could still play. A lot of people were saying we should go with someone else, someone younger, but Craig deserved to be the number one guy that year. He had a great year for us, and I know I appreciated it, being my first year in Denver. Craig was just a very smart quarterback. He always was, but in his earlier years, he was so big and could throw the ball so hard. In a way, he had to tone things down a little with his natural ability. With experience, he became just a very smart player who didn't beat himself. Sometimes the ball would go to the other team, but he didn't make many mental mistakes, and that's what you really want out of a quarterback."

## Dan Reeves: "Froggy"

A lot of ex-Broncos do dead-on impressions of Dan Reeves. His South Carolina accent was so thick, people had to listen hard to understand every word he said. But who was Dan Reeves? He was a lot of things to a lot of people, but above all it can't be said he wasn't a winner.

Red Miller was fired by new owner Edgar Kaiser, but Morton was kept around despite some of the turmoil over playing time and other disagreements with Miller.

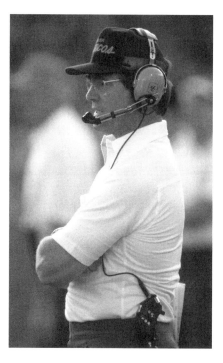

*Known as "Frog" for his stance as a player, head coach Dan Reeves brought intelligence, respect, and Super Bowl experience to his position in 1981.*

Reeves, Morton said, never had the greatest offensive ability, but was always the smartest player on the field.

"He knew the game inside and out, and that's how he got through. Even with that goofy frog stance he had as a player. They tried him at every position, but he just kept moving around. Personally, Danny was just the greatest guy. He is certainly one of my favorite people, and one of my dearest friends. When he first came to the Broncos, I remember telling him, though, 'Hey, Denver is a little further north of Dallas, and certainly South Carolina or Georgia,' where he used to live and play. The thing was, you couldn't understand a word he said, with that accent of his. I worried a little about how he would adapt to a place like Denver, but those worries were unfounded. And it was never awkward between us at all, having been teammates, but then him being the coach. Everybody knew that I was the quarterback and he was the head coach. My loyalty was to him, and trying to get his message across to the team. We never had one problem between us. I mean, we would have some arguments at times over a play on the sidelines, but that's normal and we got along great."

Reeves didn't get along as well with some of the management above him, however. One of Kaiser's first hires, as the Broncos' general manager, was a man named Hein Poulus. A former accountant, Poulus had no football operations experience, and his tenure was pilloried in the press.

"But Dan Reeves was a winner, period. He's been in so many Super Bowls, as a player and coach. He's got a great collection of some really great and really ugly rings. But he coached two different NFL teams to the Super Bowl. That's amazing. I really think he should be in the Hall of Fame as a coach. If Marv Levy can make it, losing four Super Bowls, I think Danny should be there, too."

That Morton was, and still is, great friends with Reeves might have come as a surprise to some, given what happened in the final minute of Super Bowl V. On a second-and-35 play from the Cowboys' 35-yard line, with 59 seconds left in regulation of a 13–13 game with Baltimore, Morton threw the interception that wound up costing Dallas a world championship.

However, Reeves probably should have caught the pass. Although it was thrown a little too high, Reeves had both hands on the football in front of him. While jumping for the pass, Reeves had his legs taken from under him by Baltimore cornerback Jerry Logan and bobbled the ball. Colts linebacker Mike Curtis swooped in and grabbed the floating football and ran 13 yards to the Dallas 28. Two plays later, from the Dallas 25, Jim O'Brien kicked the field goal that won the game. It was such a bitter pill for Cowboys Hall of Fame lineman Bob Lilly that, after O'Brien's kick, he flung his helmet about 30 yards down the Miami Orange Bowl field.

"One thing you never, ever wanted to do was get Bob Lilly mad, and I guess we did that with that play. Bob was just so great in that game, too. It was horrible. I never really talked about the play much with Danny. The pass was a little high. We finally were able to laugh about it, or at least talk about it, a little later on, when he got to the Broncos. We never should have thrown the ball in that situation, is the bottom line. We should have just run out the clock and played for overtime. That whole day, we just thought for sure we were going to win the football game. We played better than they did, but we just didn't get it done."

Reeves says today, "I should have caught the pass. It hit my hands. But we shouldn't have been throwing the football in that situation probably, not on third [actually, second]-and-long in the last two minutes. We learned a lesson."

Before the game, Morton's face was on a giant balloon, right next to Colts legendary quarterback Johnny Unitas. Morton said he was a little overwhelmed at that sight.

"There's me, right next to the legendary Johnny Unitas. I mean, it awed me and maybe not in a good way for me right before a game like that. I mean, he was the greatest quarterback of all time and there's me. It was, and still is, one of the strangest, weirdest moments of my whole life, seeing that balloon."

Reeves couldn't believe he was a part of the sport's biggest game, either. He went undrafted out of the University of South Carolina, after starting at quarterback for three years. He managed to sign with the Cowboys as a free agent. Coach Tom Landry liked him enough to give him a job, but only as a halfback. He played eight years with the Cowboys, but started only eight games. In 1970, he became one of the first player-coaches in NFL history, but coached much more than he played.

Reeves hated the coaching job. Teammates such as Bullet Bob Hayes wouldn't listen to him and he felt like he might have gotten the job out of charity. So, after the 1972 season, he quit to sell real estate. The Cowboys lured him back a few years later, though, and this time he felt more at home as a coach.

He landed the Bronco job in '81, and enjoyed a fine 10–6 record, with his old teammate leading the way.

## 1981—The Last Year. The Best Year

When you take a look at Craig Morton's career statistics, one of the first questions that comes to mind is: why did he retire in

1982? Especially, after he had the best statistical season of his career the year before?

Morton threw for 3,195 yards in 1981, with 225 completions and 21 touchdown passes. Those are all career highs. One year later, however, he was out of football.

The questions remain: How did he have his best statistical year, at age 38, and why did it end so soon after that?

"As far as why I had the best numbers year ever, I have no clue. All I know is that I was comfortable in that offense, with Danny Reeves as coach. I knew that he wanted to open things up more. And, we had a real good crop of young receivers that were just coming up, guys like Steve Watson, and we also started to throw a lot more screens out of the backfield and shorter patterns like that. The game was starting to change a little, with shorter patterns overall.

"But otherwise, I don't remember that year very fondly, all because of our last game. It was at Chicago, and we needed to win to get into the playoffs. But we lost, 35–24. We needed to rely on San Diego losing to somebody after our game, for us to get in, and that didn't happen. It was a horrible deal. I threw a couple of big interceptions that they ran back, and it was as devastating a loss as I've ever had, other than the Super Bowls. It was just a horrible loss, with no excuse. How could we play so well all year and then go there and this Bears team, which wasn't very good, beat us?

"But one thing that I always remember Don Meredith saying, was when you got your schedule for that year to look to see if you have to play Cleveland, Buffalo, Chicago, or Minnesota at the end of the year. You're going to be screwed. The chances were that they were not going to be in the playoffs, it was going to be cold out, and they were just going to relish the chance to kick your ass. But for us to lose that game was just inexplicable."

Broncos coach Dan Reeves agreed Morton was not at his best that day, but might have had a good excuse.

"He was sick with the flu," Reeves recalls. "He didn't practice all week, I don't think. Then, we have to go up against Buddy Ryan's '46 Defense' and it just wasn't a good day for us."

No excuses, Morton said.

"The bottom line is, I was horseshit. If I was good enough to put on the uniform, then I should have been good enough to play a good game."

## The Last Game

Craig Morton's last game in the NFL came on September 19, 1982, at Mile High Stadium against the San Francisco 49ers. There were plenty of ironies about the day.

For starters, Morton played against the team he grew up idolizing. He played against the coach, Bill Walsh, who helped recruit him to California-Berkeley. And, on the week before the game, his alma mater made a rare trip to Boulder, Colorado, to play against the Colorado Buffaloes. The Golden Bears prevailed 31-17 under new coach Joe Kapp, who Morton grew up really idolizing after watching him play at Memorial Field. Morton went to the Cal-CU game, and hugged Kapp afterward in the locker room. Kapp introduced Morton as the "most underrated quarterback in the history of the game."

Against the 49ers, Morton played only part of one quarter, finishing 3-for-4 passing for 40 yards and one interception. He suffered a slight groin pull and was replaced by Steve DeBerg.

Morton wasn't sure it was going to be his last game. And it probably wouldn't have been, if not for a players strike that began two days afterward. During the strike, Morton had knee surgery, but didn't feel right when the strike was over and decided to retire.

"Now that I think back to that final weekend that I played, it kind of hits home how a lot of things came full circle for me, with Cal playing up the road, and playing against the 49ers and Bill Walsh. These were some people really close to me, people like Walsh and Joe Kapp. Joe Kapp used to hang out around my house when I was in high school, trying to recruit me to Cal. But the second time he came to my house, I had decided to go to Stanford. My mom came to me and said 'Joe's outside' and I told her to tell him I wasn't home. But I ended up going out there and

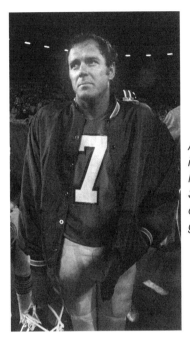

*After suffering a groin pull and an increasingly agitated knee, Craig Morton watched from the sidelines on September 19, 1982. It would turn out to be his last professional football game.*

we started talking, and he said, 'You're not a Stanford guy. You're a Bear, you're always going to be a Bear.' And he was right. I still see Joe a lot, and he's just one of my favorite people."

About the strike that effectively decided the end of his career, Morton said the vast majority of players didn't want to do it. But they felt pressured into it.

"I was railing against it, because I didn't think anything would change. I just always hated the strong-arm tactics by some people in the union. (Current NFLPA president) Gene Upshaw wrote me a letter one time, after I came out against it. He was still playing for the Raiders at the time, and he said, 'There's no place in football for players like you, and wait 'til we get out on the football field,' kind of a threat. I wrote him back and said, 'Ah, hey Gene, both of us play offense. You're not going to do anything to me.' But they got all the young guys to vote for the strike. You just can't strike in pro sports. It's not like the bus drivers going on strike or some-thing. Players never win in a strike. They always lose, and we lost in that deal that year."

# chapter 3
# The Formative Years

*"…I went to Cal for a banquet, and was blown away by the pride and enthusiasm they had for the program and I just said this was the place I wanted to be."*

—Craig Morton

## Growing Up

Larry Craig Morton was born February 5, 1943, in Flint, Michigan, and would have two younger sisters, Sharon and Sandy. Morton's father, Ken, served as a sergeant in World War II, mostly in New Guinea, and found work as a glassblower after returning. His mother, Maxine, worked as a school administrator. Morton recalls an apple-pie childhood, playing sports all day, especially after the family moved to Campbell, Calif., just south of San Francisco, when he was about five.

But it wasn't all fun and games. Ken Morton, like many men of his generation, didn't show affection or emotion very easily, especially after he returned from the war. He was a strict man, a disciplinarian, who had little time for excuses. Craig Morton loved his father, but that doesn't mean there wasn't plenty of tension between them.

"My mom said he was the greatest guy in the world, but when he came back from the war, he was different. He never talked to me about anything about his war experiences. He went in as an enlisted man and came out as a captain, so he got a lot of battle-field promotions. Now, all I watch is The History Channel, especially when WWII is the topic. It's so I can learn more about what my dad went through, and (why) we went through shit. He just went through unbelievable hell, and he absolutely hated the Japanese, forever. My mom told me a story one time, when he came home on leave when I was born. When he came home, he just had no patience at all. She said that the worst moment of her life was when he went to my crib, where I was crying, and he wanted me to be quiet, and he spanked me.

"My dad, he pushed me. He was the most firm, strict father there was. But now that I look back, he also knew what was best for me at the time. I loved him to death, but I feared him so much. He was a hero in the war, though, and I feel the same about our troops now. They're all heroes.

*His exemplary athletic abilities combined with a strict father and upbringing helped mold Craig Morton into the strong, focused man he is today.*

My father was a good baseball player, and he got a tryout with the St. Louis Cardinals. He was a catcher. He loved my sports and that I was good, but he never complimented me on it.

"Otherwise, growing up in Campbell was great. It was a town of about 8,000 people, right in the middle of the prune and apricot capital of the world. All my life I had the greatest coaches and teachers ever to help me. It was the best place ever. I still remember Mrs. Smith, my fifth and sixth grade teacher. Bruce Stevenson was my first grade-school coach, and we're still very good friends to this day. I can't emphasize enough how good it was for me to have the coaches and teachers that I did. Everything in Campbell just revolved around the community. They had the old Settlers Day parade, and I got to ride in a car in that parade when I was in fourth grade, and every summer I would pick prunes and apricots. That wasn't very much fun, but it was what you did, and really was good stuff overall.

"My mother was just the opposite of my dad, just the kindest person in the world. My dad worked hard at his job. He would take me to his shop and he would make these amazing little birds and neon signs, and was just a very talented man.

"I was good at sports pretty much right away. Jim Muir was my football coach in high school, Bert Robinson was the basketball coach, and John Oldom was my baseball coach. I was all-state in football, baseball, and basketball. I started to get a real formulation about what I wanted to do with my life, which was athletics. I was just always in a play yard somewhere, or a field, just playing ball. When I talk to kids today, I always tell them, 'You've got to get out there in the play yards if you want to get good.' Back in my day, you never spent any time indoors. First of all, the houses were too small, and all you'd do is just go in to have dinner with everybody. Otherwise, it was always outside to play ball with my buddies.

Things started to get very tense between Morton and his father around his freshman year of high school. It wasn't long before Morton would stand up to his father, challenging him to a physical confrontation.

"I was always an 'A' student, and in my freshman year of high school I got a 'C' in English and he grounded me basically for four years. I was in my room every night at 7 o'clock, five nights a week. And I probably did worse in school because of that, because I was so upset every night. Then, my senior year, I said, 'Dad, I'm not doing this anymore.' And he said, 'Is that right, young man?' And I said, 'Yup, and if you want to do something about it, let's go.'

I think every young man, if he's got an asshole dad, he's finally got to stand up to him. He just looked at me. And I just left, ran out of the house. When I came back, my mom was up and that my dad said that I was leaving, and what a dumb-ass trick it was that I played. So, I wrote him a long letter, saying I was sorry and not going to do that. But also that I'm not spending my life in my room, just because I got a 'C.' I could get into any college I wanted to at the time (Morton had more than 30 scholarship offers to top schools because of his athletic prowess). I didn't know if he was going to fight me or not. I was 18 at the time. I was a wrestler, too, so I know I could handle him. I remember at a picnic once, my uncle said 'let's wrestle' and I pinned him in about three minutes. And I remember my dad looking like, 'Hmmm, he's got some strength.' So, if my dad got up out of his chair, I knew what I was going to do. He had no chance, but that didn't mean that you weren't fearful. It was just a scary time. Things were always tough between him and my mom, and a boy always loves his mom more than anything, so I always took her side. I remember hearing her cry from the bathroom one time, when I was 16 or so, and I asked what was wrong, and he'd hit her. I went ballistic. I told him that if he ever touched her again, he'd be sorry. But they survived it, although they separated one time when I was in college. I remember my dad being so weak. He called me and said 'I need to talk to you, can you come home son?', but I just didn't know this person. He just didn't know what to do without my mom. He said, 'You've got to call her,' and I said I couldn't do that, and that he had to do it, that he had to change his ways. He would start telling me some personal stuff between them, and I didn't want to hear that stuff. I just told him he had to stop being an ass.

"And he started to treat me a little better. We never fought. But it was still a long time before we could really show any kind of affection for one another. I didn't hug my dad for the first time until my own son was about 3, in 1982, right after I'd retired. He was still being tough, and was even that way with my son, Michael. His deal was always saying 'Young man, get in that door or I'm going to wear your pants out' and I said, 'Dad, don't you ever say that to him again.' I just said, 'Why don't you talk to him with love, how come you can't love him?' He said, 'I do' and I said, 'Well, don't threaten him.' And then I said, 'Come here,' and I forced my dad to hug me. He hugged me, and from then on, he loved doing that. It took a long time.

"I've always kissed my kids right on the lips when I see them. I don't care. I just do that. The main thing I took away from my dad was that I was never going to be like him. There's no question that he loved me, but I decided I was going to be demonstrative with my affection for my kids. And that's the way it's been."

## The Cal Years

Morton was one of the country's most sought-after athletes coming out of Campbell High School in 1961, and not just for football. Campbell was a powerhouse in every sport, winning just about every state title in Morton's senior year, largely because of him.

He seriously considered a career in baseball, and actually received a combination baseball-football scholarship at the University of California-Berkeley.

Before becoming a Golden Bear, however, he promised his dad he would take a look at Notre Dame first. Despite being hosted by Daryle Lamonica, he felt most comfortable with the nearby Golden Bears program, which was coached by Marv Levy, who would go on to coach the Buffalo Bills to four Super Bowls. The main recruiter for the Golden Bears, however, was a Levy assistant named Bill Walsh.

Morton had a superb career at Cal; good enough that he one day would be selected to the College Football Hall of Fame. The problem was, Morton didn't have a lot of other talent around him and he never had a winning season with the Golden Bears, despite being an All-American in 1964, finishing seventh in the Heisman Trophy voting. Wearing No. 4, Morton had a 8–21–1 record at Cal, completing 355 of 641 passes for 4,501 yards and 36 touchdown passes.

"Actually, I was going to first go to Stanford. But Marv Levy was the coach, and I went to Cal for a banquet, and was blown away by the pride and enthusiasm they had for the program and I just said this was the place I wanted to be. Things didn't start so great on the field, though. Levy wanted to see who the tough guys were, so at spring practice he had me return some punts, and I lasted about three returns before I tore my knee up. I wondered if

I made a mistake. They wanted me to redshirt, but I said no, I was going to keep going. My first game was against Penn State, No. 2 in the country. Marv puts me in at the half, and I ended up breaking up every Cal record in passing in that one half. We ended up losing by two points (23–21) and nearly had the upset of the year. I wish I'd played the first half."

It wasn't long, though, before Morton got a radically different view of life, with the accent on radical. These were the 1960s, after all, and Berkeley was in the center of the free speech movement, led mainly by a student named Mario Savio. Morton, however, served in the ROTC, and his politics were right of center. Still, he developed a great admiration for President John F. Kennedy after he gave a speech at Cal. Morton was a junior when Kennedy was assassinated, and like everybody else who was old enough at the time, he remembers exactly where he was.

"I was coming out of a speech class, and everybody was crying. I wondered what was going on, then somebody said it to me and I remember feeling numb. They canceled our game that weekend (unlike the NFL, which played games that weekend), and it was a horrible deal. Also, the Vietnam War was going on, and Cal just started to become a different place. I wasn't in school when all the riots started happening (in 1970), but the beginnings of it was there during my years.

"To me, Mario Savio was leading what I didn't think was a free speech movement, but just the start of the radical movement. When I was at school, everybody had their little soap box. But it got to be if they felt like the whole school wasn't listening to them, then their constitutional rights were being violated, which was never the case. It just kept going on and on. I guess I wasn't part of the hippie movement. I had long hair once, but it was so ugly that it didn't last long. I guess I've always been to the conservative side of the political spectrum. But I like to think I'm an independent in a lot of ways. I try to evaluate everything I look at objectively."

## That First Big Check

Craig Morton used to always notice the gleaming, gold Jaguar just up the street from his college dorm room. Not that he'd ever get to own such a car, but there was no law against looking, and the Cal senior could only drool at the its magnificence.

That is, until the wonderful day when he signed his first contract with the Dallas Cowboys in 1965, the year he was drafted. Morton got a big-money deal for the times, and also got them to throw in the Jaguar as a bonus.

"My first pro contract was for $150,000, and an XKE. That was a three-year contract, the money, plus the car. I used to go by that Jaguar dealership probably twice a week as a senior. I thought I was dreaming thinking I could get it. But (in) the original contract with Dallas, the car was part of the deal. It was one of the great moments of my life being able to walk into that dealership and say, 'That's mine' without having to pay a cent for it.

"Also, when I signed with the Cowboys, I got a bonus check for $25,000. I just got it and put it in the bank, although I don't think it lasted long (partying) with my friends and everything.

"But we had so much fun with that Jaguar. My friends still remind me of the times when I just gave them the car. I'd just say 'take the keys' and let them have fun. There's a guy named Bill Harlan, a guy who now owns one of the biggest wineries in Napa Valley, and I was friends with him back then, and he still tells me it was one of the best things of his whole life, when I'd give him the keys to the car and tell him to have a great time."

Little did Morton realize, however, that driving a Jag in Dallas in summer would be like driving a sauna on wheels.

"The car had no air conditioning. So, I drove it for about a week in Dallas, and I had to sell it in a week. It was so humid and hot. You just couldn't drive it in that heat. So, I had to trade in my dream car after about four or five months, for a T-Bird that had one of those roofs that folded down in the trunk. So, it was a good trade, but it was nothing like the XKE. There will never be another car like that one."

Today, Morton tools around the Berkeley campus in a used Mercedes.

"Unbelievable machine," he says. "Not as flashy as that old Jag, but a lot more reliable and cooler in the heat."

# chapter 4
# Teammates

*"On the field, he was a guy who always made something happen. He would hit somebody and cause a fumble or he'd recover a fumble. I loved him as a teammate. He wanted just to win."*

—Craig Morton on Broncos teammate Lyle Alzado

Eighteen years in the NFL meant Craig Morton played with a lot of different people. An entire book could be written about all the zany characters he played with in Dallas. Don Meredith was certainly one. Dandy Don lived life on his terms, and that meant having a good time. He is probably better known to the public as the color man on ABC's *Monday Night Football* in the 1970s, alongside Frank Gifford and the bombastic Howard Cosell. His singing of "Turn out the Lights, the Party's Over" became one of Meredith's signature moments when the game was decided.

This book primarily focuses on Morton's Bronco teammates, and while there may not have been any to rival the color of Dandy Don or *North Dallas Forty* author, Peter Gent, there were certainly many unique characters.

## Lyle Alzado: One Of A Kind

When Morton got to Denver, he obviously had a lot of new teammates to get to know. Several of them were already established NFL players, and popular with the Denver fans. Probably nobody was more popular entering the 1977 season than defensive lineman Lyle Alzado.

Growing up on the tough streets of Brooklyn, Alzado had a brash, outspoken, fighter's mentality. He seriously considered leaving the NFL for a boxing career, after a 1979 exhibition fight with heavyweight champ Muhammad Ali at Mile High Stadium.

Alzado's life seemed like a fairy tale. A little-known high school player, small-time college player who somehow made it to the big time as an NFL star. But in 1991, Alzado admitted in a first-person story to *Sports Illustrated* that throughout his career, he was a voracious user of steroids and human growth hormone. He believed it was why he developed brain cancer, and by the time of his death at age 43 in 1992, he regularly cautioned kids and anybody else that steroids were no good.

Fifteen years after Alzado's death, Morton remembers a complex, conflicted man whose volcanic temper hid what he

*Brash and outspoken and a one-time boxer against Muhammad Ali, Lyle Alzado was described as a voracious competitor, yet a genuine friend by those who knew him best. Alzado worked to educate children about the harmful affects of steroids before his death in 1992.* Photo courtesy of AP Images.

believes was the real person: a champion of the underdog and a generous soul, especially toward children.

"Lyle was the kind of guy, every time I came into the locker room, I didn't know what kind of mood he was going to be in. He was right across from me in the locker room, and it was always like, 'I wonder how Lyle's going to feel today?' It got to the point where you just never knew. Before games, he was always just pacing by himself, really intense.

"But he was a very, very sensitive guy. I don't know if everybody knew that about him. And although there was a lot of stuff in the air about what guys might be doing, to make themselves so buff, nobody really knew what was going on with steroids. At least I didn't. I used to go up to him and say, 'I can't believe you have such an unbelievable body like this. Give me your workout routine, would ya?' I knew a lot of guys were big from weight training, but nobody can ever have not one centimeter of fat on him. Then, all these pimples on your back. But in those days, nothing was illegal; nobody asked what these guys did.

"There were a lot of I guys I played with and against that, when they retired, I'd say I wanted to be on their diet, because they went from about 270 pounds to 220 or something. Now, you kind of know who some of those guys were, who might have been taking them.

"But Lyle was one of those guys who loved kids, and he loved the fans. After practices, we'd have 100 people waiting around for autographs, and Lyle would be the most generous guy with his time. At Christmas parties, you would always see him doing something that wouldn't necessarily be benefiting Lyle, like a lot of people thought. A lot of people thought that Lyle was a self promoter, and maybe he was at times. So what? But he was always connected with a lot of people that were in hospitals, and he did a lot of things for them that nobody knew about."

"But of course there was another side to Lyle, and that was the fighter, the hot-tempered guy. I never had any confrontations with him, and we had a very good relationship, where we talked a lot. But there were times when I'd tell him, 'Look, why are you acting like an asshole? I mean, come on, don't do this.' A couple other guys on the team had some influence on him, too, and could talk to him, guys like Barney Chavous and Rubin Carter. They would kind of protect Lyle when they knew he was going to flip out. I had many discussions about the right way to do things and I'd just say, 'This temper thing with teammates, it just doesn't work.'"

In 1972, Alzado had a fight with Broncos teammate Dwight Harrison. After the fight, which Harrison lost, he went to his truck and got his gun, returning to the locker room yelling, "Where's Lyle?" Harrison was talked out of firing the gun by Floyd Little, and Harrison was traded shortly thereafter to Buffalo in a deal that brought Haven Moses to the Broncos.

"Lyle was either on top of the world or he was totally depressed. I don't think the steroids would help in that way. I think the best time of his life in Denver, other than getting to a Super Bowl, was when he owned a nightclub in the Cherry Creek area. He had what might have been maybe the first disco in Denver at the time. It was really successful. After that, he was Mister Alzado. That was really big time for him.

On the field, he was a guy who always made something happen. He would hit somebody and cause a fumble or he'd recover a fumble. I loved him as a teammate. He wanted just to win."

At the 1979 exhibition with Ali, Morton served as an honorary corner man for Alzado. The fight lasted eight rounds, drawing a crowd of about 30,000 in the 76,000-seat stadium. The count disappointed Alzado and the promoters. Morton, a boxing fan who attended the first two Ali-Joe Frazier fights in New York, has many vivid memories of the event, especially those of Alzado thinking he really had a shot at beating The Champ.

"Lyle really thought he was going to win. I remember being in the locker room before the fight, and him saying something like, 'I got this guy, I'm gonna kick his ass.' And of course, we all just kind of looked at him funny and thought to ourselves that this guy is crazy, because Ali was just like magic in the ring. But we certainly didn't say that to Lyle, because then he'd probably try to kick our asses, too.

"Well, the fight starts, and Ali was kind of having fun, playing to the fans and letting Lyle get a couple in on him. Ali would put his arms around Lyle's waist and let Lyle get him a couple body shots. But Lyle really thought Ali was fighting hard. So he gets back to the corner and he's pumped up, telling us, 'He's mine' and things like that.

"But then Ali started to get, I think, a little ticked off at some of the stuff Lyle was doing or maybe thinking. I don't think he realized just how serious Lyle was about this, maybe thinking he was going to become the new champ of the world or something. So, of course, that's when he gave Lyle a few combinations to the head and staggered him around a little and let it be known that there was no way that Muhammad Ali was going to be shown up by Lyle Alzado.

"The fight went eight rounds, and after it was over, Lyle knew. He knew he never had any shot, that this was a guy way out of his league. But he did think he could work his way up to being a good boxer after that. And that's partly how he ended up getting traded out of Denver to Cleveland, because he used that a little bit as leverage against Broncos management, that he might turn pro as a boxer if they didn't pay him.

After Alzado was traded to the Browns following a contract dispute, he spent a couple of miserable seasons there before resurrecting his career with the Los Angeles Raiders, winning a Super Bowl in 1984. Morton saw Alzado only sporadically after that, but maintained a close personal bond to the end.

"I took Lyle to church one time in Denver, and the softest side to him I ever saw was when he walked down the aisle, for the call for those who wanted to accept Christ. I really think that affected a lot of the rest of his life. He was a born-again Christian.

"I think one of the great things about Lyle's life was that he was honest and up front in the end about what he did. He honestly said, 'Hey, wise up, don't do what I did.' He left some good life lessons, because at the time, nobody else was talking about that stuff.

"I was just very appreciative and honored that I was his teammate. My all-time favorite memory of him is after we beat the Raiders in the playoffs my first year. I was just so elated that I could play the game, first of all, because I was hurt. In the shower after the game, I was just so spent emotionally that I started crying. Lyle came over and gave me a hug and he just said, 'We did it.' He was the first guy to talk to me in the locker room, telling me we were going to win a championship now that I was there. It was phenomenal."

## The Tanqueray Judge

Because of his what his teammates kiddingly referred to as his righteous air, tight end Riley Odoms was tagged with the nickname The Judge. But Morton added a twist:

"I called him the "Tanqueray Judge," because he loved Tanqueray gin. You could smell it on him every Saturday morning, the day before a game, because he would go out on Friday night. But the Tanqueray Judge always came to play on Sunday, and he was a

*Teammates kid tight end Riley Odoms by calling him "The Judge" because of his righteous air. Morton calls him Tanqueray Judge because of his beverage of choice. History calls Odoms one of the best tight ends, earning him four trips to the Pro Bowl.*

great player. He was a great character, too, just the most fun guy. But the bottom line was he was a great receiver. He could read defenses and blitzes better than any tight end I ever played with. That's why he caught so many passes, but we got blitzed a lot, and I was always looking for him. We used to get a lot of double-zone defenses, and the linebackers couldn't keep up with Riley.

"But I always blame—well, I kid anyway—Riley for something that happened in the first quarter of the 1978 season. I was running out-of-bounds on a play that Riley either missed an assignment or didn't run the right route, and I'm saying, 'Aw shoot, this is not good.' Because when I was running, trying to get out of bounds, I could never really make it. I would get absolutely rolled up, which is never good for a quarterback. So, I'm just running for my life on this play, and I get hit, and I'm going head over tea kettle, and I land on my left shoulder and it pops. So, I'm laying there and saying, 'Son of a bitch.' I've separated my shoulder. So, as I'm walking back to the huddle, everybody is looking at me. They know I'm hurt, and wondering what I'm going to do. And I say, 'Aw f*ck it.' I go in the huddle and say, 'All right, you son of a bitches, I've popped my shoulder on the first play of the year. So you're really going to have to work your asses off, because this is going to be a long-ass year.'

"One of the things that saved me that year was that we had a water bed at the time, one of those ones with a wooden frame. So, I could sleep on my stomach at night and rest my shoulder on that wooden frame and keep it in place, so I could sleep at night. The whole year, that's what I had to deal with, because Riley didn't get open on that play. I said to him, 'No more Tanqueray for you, you stupid ass.' But I was just playing with him. The truth is, he was a real warrior on the football field. He made the Pro Bowl a few times (four overall) and might have been the best tight end of his day. I know New England had Russ Francis and there were a few other guys, like Dave Casper and Kellen Winslow a little later, but Riley might have been the best of the bunch in his day. He made things a lot easier for me. Except for that damn play where I got crushed!"

## Jim Turner: Ole High-Tops

From 1971 to 1979, Jim Turner was the place-kicker for the Broncos. He came in a trade in 1971 from the New York Jets, for Bobby Howfield, winning a Super Bowl with the Jets in 1969. Turner scored 10 of New York's 16 points, in the famous 16–7 victory over the favored Baltimore Colts.

Turner was inducted into the Broncos' Ring of Fame the same year as Morton. While Morton calls Turner a well-respected teammate, he said not many knew well the kicker who wore black high-top shoes.

"He was a bit of an enigma. If I can call myself one as a player, he certainly was one, too. There were some sides to him that people didn't really know too well probably off the team. But I tell you what, as funny as he looked in those high-tops, and they do look funny, he was like a machine as a kicker. He just came out there and drilled the ball through the uprights and you never had to worry about him. And I'll just never forget him catching that pass in Oakland, in 1977, for a touchdown. He left no doubt as to who the slowest player on the team was on that play. But he got into the end zone. That was Jim as a player: just very dogged and determined. But off the field, you didn't get to know Jim all that well, even though I liked what I did know of him. But he's a guy I'm proud to have played with."

Turner went on to host a radio talk show for years in Denver, and became a tireless advocate of at-risk kids. He mentored hundreds of young kids in the area, and received several humanitarian awards.

## Big Barney

Defensive lineman Barney Chavous was a mainstay on all the excellent Broncos teams of the late 1970s. Morton remembers a great teammate, despite never being able to understand much of what he ever said.

"Barney always called me Moo-ton. He was from South Carolina. He just had a real accent, and what a character he was. Nobody, frankly, could understand a word he said. The natural deal to do with him was just laugh, but he was a big part of our defense. We had a three-man front and he was right there making plays every single down, and he got a lot of big sacks for us. He was and is a very generous guy, too, always there with a dollar for someone or a piece of advice or just a friendly ear. He's another guy from the Broncos years for me, where I just think, 'What a good guy and teammate he was.' There were just a lot of good people on those teams, not just good players, but good people. I really think that's partly why we were a successful team, because we had guys who were smart and good of character, and who just wanted to work hard and succeed. There was just very little ego on those teams, and Barney was Exhibit A of that kind of guy we had."

Chavous did some coaching with the Broncos after retiring in 1985 before moving back to South Carolina and taking up farming.


## Talkative Tom Jackson

Maybe it is no surprise, certainly not to Morton, that Tom Jackson made it as a television football analyst after his playing days.

The Broncos linebacker was not only a standout player, he might have been the best trash talker in the NFL in his day.

"If you were the opposition, he never shut up. He was on your ass from the minute the game started. He knew everything about everybody. He knew football like few others, too. But he was a trash talker, especially against Oakland. That's why I always looked forward to playing them, because I knew Tom would be going at it with (Raiders coach) John Madden. Jackson would always call him The Fat Man. He would make it from the minute the game started to say, 'Hey Fat Man.' He would not stop. And he would really get Madden's ire up a little bit. He would just yell that to him every time he ran by their sideline.

"But Tom was a great football player. And he really wasn't all that big for a linebacker, but he was just so smart on the field and was tough as nails and was very quick. He was a real playmaker for our defense, always scooping up fumbles and making big interceptions. I still remember him constantly saying, 'Do they believe in us now, do they believe in us now?' after we beat the Raiders in the '77 playoffs. He was very intense as a player, always analyzing the game and trying to think of new ways to make plays. That's why he ended up on television, talking about football after his career was over. You could never stop him from talking football."

## Rubin Carter: The Smart Man

Rubin Carter was the Broncos' nose tackle from 1975 to 1986, playing more games at the position (152) than any other at his position upon his retirement. One of his biggest moments of fame came when he landed on the cover of *Sports Illustrated* for a story headlined "The Case for the 3–4 Defense." Carter anchored the middle of that three-man front, and cited him as a textbook example of the kind of player needed for the new defensive philosophy coming into the NFL.

Carter went on to a long career in coaching, in the college and pro ranks, which doesn't surprise Morton.

"He was a very articulate guy. Very smart. He was just a class guy. He was and is a beautiful person. He was a real strong force on our team, in a quiet way. He was just a real strength-of-character kind of guy, and he really rubbed off in a positive way to so many of us. It's no surprise he's done well as a coach for a long time since he quit playing. Typical of those real sweet guys off the field, Rubin was an absolute nightmare to play against on the field. He would really go after guys. He was a bulldog type, who just wouldn't give up on a play or a game, no matter what. Most people only talk about the linebackers from those great defensive teams we had, or Alzado. But Rubin Carter was absolutely an essential part of our success."

## Billy Bryan: Tough Guy

In 1977, the Broncos took an offensive lineman out of Boston College named Steve Schindler with their first pick in the draft (18th overall). They took an offensive lineman out of Duke in the fourth round named Billy Bryan.

Bryan turned out to be the much better player for Denver. Morton remembers hearing about the supposedly huge and talented Schindler, only to see him in his first training camp and wonder who messed up.

"I mean, they said he was about 6'4", 265 [pounds], and he was about 6'1" and nowhere near 265. We went down to see the line drills and see what our No. 1 draft choice was going to do and he got his ass kicked, and Billy Bryan was in charge of it all. He would be laughing, just driving his helmet and whole body into the ground. And, I really felt sorry for Schindler, and said a couple of words to him, but he just never had a chance. But Billy was just a great player, tough as hell. But he was the guy drafted a lot lower. They just got it wrong on (Schindler). Things just weren't as sophisticated then as today when it comes to drafting. Billy Bryan was just a hell of a player and you would have thought he was the No. 1 pick, for sure.

Bryan played through the 1986 season with the Broncos, even starting in the famous "The Drive" touchdown by John Elway in the AFC Championship Game that year, in Cleveland. The player snapping to the ball to Elway in the shotgun for several of those plays on the game-tying drive was Bryan.

## The Scooter

One of Morton's favorite teammates with the Broncos was running back Rob Lytle. While Lytle's nickname was Scooter, Morton called him The Scooter Pervert, for reasons Morton doesn't even seem clear on. Morton gave a lot of nicknames he was never quite sure why.

*Known as a jokester in the locker room, Rob Lytle is all business on the field. Lytle scored the only touchdown the Broncos had in Super Bowl XII.* Photo courtesy of WireImages.

"He was not any kind of perverted guy at all. But I just called him that. I called him that out of affection. Sometimes the worse a nickname seems that you give to a guy, the more you like him. Lytle was just a tough son of a bitch, and a class guy all the way. He just took the football and ran it as hard as he could. He wasn't the fastest guy in the league, but he got the tough yards every time. The Scooter Pervert was just one of those guys that every winning team needs. He would run through a brick wall if he had to for his team."

Lytle came out of Michigan with much fanfare. He finished third in the Heisman Trophy balloting in 1976, setting a then-Wolverines record with 1,469 yards rushing. He was drafted by Denver in the second round, 45th overall, and played with the Broncos until 1983. Lytle scored the only touchdown the Broncos had in Super Bowl XII. To that point, no rookies had ever scored in a Super Bowl, but he and Dallas' Tony Dorsett did it that day.

Lytle got into the construction business following his playing career, for a company that built several football stadiums. One of them was Invesco Field at Mile High Stadium.

## Two Tickets To Lumpty-ville

One of the little known facts about the 1977 AFC Champion Broncos was the team song that was sung in the locker room after victories. It was a little ditty called "Two Tickets to Lumpty-ville."

Morton explains:

"We had an offensive lineman named Glenn Hyde, and his nickname was "Lumpty-Dumpty." So, somehow we took the song "Two Tickets to Paradise" (by Eddie Money) and turned that into "Two Tickets to Lumpty-ville" and that became pretty much our team theme song. We'd all go stand by his locker and sing it.

"That became our team song until (running back) Jon Keyworth decided he thought he could sing and put out a song called "Make Those Miracles Happen." I think that thing sold something like 50,000 copies in Colorado. It was played every single minute on the radio."

Morton was not always singing the praises of Hyde, however.

"We almost had it out a couple times. Because he was just always so fired up, and he would always be yelling in the huddle, 'P-12 Trap, P-12 Trap,' which was a play where he had a good angle over the guy he was going up against over the center. So, it was a play where it was easy for him to make a block. So one time I said, 'All right, son of a bitch. We're going to call the P-12 Trap and we better make some yards.' Well, we got stopped for like no gain and I said 'Shut…the…hell…up.' Everybody in the huddle kind of agreed with me."

## Otis Armstrong—Mr. Cool

The Broncos had one of the NFL's best running backs in the late 1960s and early '70s in Floyd Little. His heir apparent was Otis Armstrong, who came to the Broncos in 1973 as the all-time leading rusher in Purdue history.

In his second pro season Armstrong led the NFL in rushing, with 1,407 yards. But by the time Morton came to the Broncos, Armstrong's body had already started to give out on him. He had several leg injuries, and an impinged spinal cord finally forced him to retire in 1980.

After another 1,000-yard season in 1976, Armstrong never ran for more than 500 again. But Morton remembers Armstrong for his always-upbeat attitude and how it helped keep the Broncos locker room loose.

"I loved all my teammates, but Otis was just great. He was Mr. Cool, always strutting around, with a fake cigarette all the time. Every time I see him now, I just start laughing, because I know he's going to fake blowing smoke out of his mouth to me. And he was just funny as hell. He did some great impersonations. He did a great Muhammad Ali. He would do Ali pretending to talk to Alzado, when they had their fight together, and it was hysterical.

He was just always hurt a lot when I was there. But when it came down to it in our championship games, he really played well.

He was always strutting and wearing the hats and knew where the parties were, but deep down he is just a gentle soul. A great guy, and a great talent."

## Bob Swenson—Mr. Underrated

Bob Swenson was a pretty well-known player with the Broncos in his near decade stint with the team. But outside of Denver, the linebacker who also played at Morton's college alma mater did not get a lot of recognition. To Morton, Swenson was one of the best players of his time.

"He was the most underrated strong-side linebacker in football. He really was one of the great players of all time. What Swenson was really a master at was holding up the other team's tight end off the line of scrimmage. He could handle anybody at the time—The Ghost (Dave Casper) or anybody, and there were some great tight ends in that time. The first thing any great defense needs to do is control the tight end. Any coach will tell you that. You ask those guys who played against him, and they'll tell you Swenson was one of the toughest guys of all time."

## Randy Gradishar—Why not in the Hall?

One way to easily get Morton and his former Bronco teammates fired up is to mention that middle linebacker Randy Gradishar still isn't in the Pro Football Hall of Fame.

Despite never missing a game in his NFL career, from 1974 to 1983, despite being a multiple Pro Bowl player and one of the greatest college football players to ever play (at Ohio State) Gradishar's credentials somehow were not good enough for the selection committee.

"It's bullshit. Pure bullshit. He was a great, great football player, the total leader of our defense. Off the field, he was the nicest guy you'd ever want to meet, but, boy, you get him on a football field and he would knock your ass off.

"I remember so many fourth-and-1s for the opposing team, where Randy would just come up and stop them cold. He was incredible. He should be in the Hall of Fame without any question. He was one of the greatest players I've ever played with or against, and I played with a lot of great ones. It's a shame he's not in the Hall and it's a joke. On a great—and I mean, great—defense, he was the leader of the whole gang. I still can't believe not one of those guys from that great defense is in Canton, Ohio. What a joke."

It was speculated in the Denver papers in early 2008 that Gradishar might finally make it to the Hall of Fame. He was a finalist in his 20th and final year of eligibility, and there seemed to be a groundswell to give No. 53 the justice he deserved. Alas, Gradishar was passed over one final time, to renewed outrage from all who played with him.

His only hope remained inclusion from the NFL Veteran's Committee, a long shot at best.

"There just seems to be some kind of political crap that has kept Randy out," kicker Jim Turner said. "It'll never make sense why he's not in still."

## Louis Wright—None Better

Louis Wright was named an All-Pro eight times in his Bronco career, and went to the Pro Bowl five times. But he's another great Bronco defensive player who still hasn't made it to the Pro Football Hall of Fame.

Morton feels as strongly about that as he does about Randy Gradishar. Wright played cornerback from 1975 to 1986, and Morton believes nobody was ever better.

"I'd played with a cornerback in Dallas named Mel Renfro and, later, Herb Adderley. And, I'd played against some great ones, too. But when I saw Louis Wright, he was as good as any of them, and he's as good as anybody who's ever played the game. He had such great instincts. And he was always such a fun guy. He was Boog-a-loo to me, because I just loved the way he could get down and dance. Wow, what an amazing player. He was always the fun guy that never caused any problems. He was always smiling. He reminded me a little bit of (musician) Chuck Berry. He was just always having a great time, and just had so much talent. I tell you, these cornerbacks in the Hall of Fame right now, they are not better than Louis Wright. Denver just doesn't get the respect it deserves from the Hall. That defense, you could have had several guys in there. Louis is right there at the top of the list."

## Haven Moses—The Other 'M'

Haven Moses was establishing himself as a pretty good NFL receiver with the Buffalo Bills by the time he was traded to the Broncos after five games of the 1972 season. He was traded for a player named Dwight Harrison, who nearly went down in infamy after pulling a gun on Lyle Alzado in the Bronco locker room following a physical altercation. After being talked down by Bronco teammates Floyd Little and Jim Turner, Harrison was traded that night by John Ralston to the Bills for Moses.

Moses was even more established as a good pass catcher when Morton came to the Broncos in 1977.

But Moses had never played with a quarterback with Morton's skill and smarts. It had been a while since Morton had a receiver of Moses' caliber, and so when they became teammates, a great bond developed on the field. Soon, the press came up with the nickname for the two: the M&M Connection. Today, a poster bearing the nickname and featuring the two in action is a somewhat valuable commodity on eBay, and the two have remained close. Moses suffered a stroke in 2003 and lost much of the motor skills on his left side. But he has made substantial progress since, and his speech wasn't affected. Still, Morton has difficulty not becoming emotional when talking about No. 25, the other half of Denver's best-known connection of the late '70s.

"It was definitely something almost eerie, how well Haven and I read each other on the field. Haven knew exactly what I saw from my position, to where he had to be, and where the ball was going to be. He saw the field the same way I did. He also had amazing hands—and I do mean amazing. He was born with webbed hands, in that they were curled a bit. He could never straighten his hands out. They were kind of naturally curved, to be able to catch a football. There were so many times when I would just throw the ball and know he'd be right where it ended up. What a receiver he was, and a good friend. The stroke really threw a lot of us for a loop when it happened, but he's battled that thing just like any cornerback he ever faced in the NFL. And just like those cornerbacks, he's kicking their ass."

## The Blade

Steve Watson, nicknamed The Blade, came to the Broncos in 1979, after a college career at Temple. He was known for his slashing running style and ability to cut across the middle.

He became a Pro Bowl receiver, and a favorite target of Morton's in his last full year, 1981. One of the passes they connected with that year was for 95 yards, in San Diego.

"I remember seeing him for the first time in mini-camp, and being amazed that anybody so tall and so fast could also have such great control of his body. I went up to some of our coaches and said, 'I don't know what you guys are thinking with this guy, but you keep him.' This was before the regular training camp, so you didn't know what their plans were, but he was a keeper. Nobody who is 6'4" like he is can run like him. He was the best receiver I ever played with at running over the middle. He was fearless. There was a game in Buffalo his first year, where I threw to him in the last minute and we won the game on a field goal (19–16, on December 2), and it was just a play that I called and basically just drew it up in the dirt and said, 'Okay

Blade, you just get to this spot here and the ball will be there for you when you turn around, and then Turner will come in and kick the field goal and we'll go home.' Watson made a great play around Isiah Robertson, who was a great linebacker at the time, and the play went just as planned. Turner came in, kicked the field goal, and we had a great victory in this awful, snowy day. Except that Red Miller was pissed off as hell, because he had nothing to do with the play. We're running off the field and not really even celebrating, because Red is so mad. I don't think anybody even congratulated Turner after the kick even. It was amazing."

## Studley

Dave Studdard was one anchor of Broncos offensive lines through the 1980s, protecting both Morton and John Elway in his career.

Morton remembers a "good old Texas boy" who was a kind soul and tremendous player.

"I loved Studley. I always loved my offensive linemen, but Studley was very special. Every year, I would always have all the offensive linemen over to my house, and have dinner for them sometimes during the year. But Studley and I became close very quickly. Our families took vacations together, and he was so much fun. He was a tough son of a bitch, too. It says a lot about him that he became one of Elway's favorites, too. I know they became very close as well. He was kind of the leader of the offensive line. Guys did what he said. Whether it was having a couple of beers or where they were going to dinner or what kind of thing they might want to try on the field, he led the way. Offensive linemen are always really close, generally. They have to be. The one thing I never quite understood was O-line guys always thought they had to drink about 20 beers the night before a game."

## The Gentle Giant

Bring up the name Claudie Minor to Morton and you notice the affection in his voice. Minor, one of the bigger players in his day and offensive line standout, played a mean game on the field and lived a quiet life off it.

"He was the gentle giant. He was always 280–285 pounds, and they always said, 'you can't be that heavy.' And some of our other players would have trouble maintaining what was supposed to be the proper weight, which I always thought was a BS tradition of football whose time had come and gone. So, to make weight, which was every Thursday morning at the practice field, some guys would go to a hotel that was right across the street. And they would get there at about 5 a.m. and basically sweat 10–15 pounds off. They'd go to the whirlpool, then a sauna. So, you'd have Good Gawdy, Miss Claudie, the Tanqueray Judge, Norris Weese, and Penrose every once in a while because these guys could never make weight. If they didn't, the fine was something like 50 dollars for every pound over. So, if you're 10 pounds over every week, it's a lot of money. To me, this was despicable, that they made these (players) come in every Thursday to make weigh in, just to meet some artificial number. I don't think it was very good for their bodies, and Claudie would seem sick at practice every Thursday because of this stuff. And then right after the weigh in, before practice, these guys would all have the biggest bags of food you've ever seen by their locker and they would eat that 15 pounds back. But I really think this hurt these guys in the long haul. Today, they don't do things like that anymore. Assistant coach Stan Jones was always the guy who had to do the weigh-ins, and I would go up to him and say, 'Why the hell are we doing this Stan, this is killing some of these guys and it's not helping their performance at all. It's hurting them and our team.' And he would just say, 'Well, this is what Red wants.'

But Claudie was just such a kind person, and a great right tackle. He was just such a big-framed guy. His playing weight should have been 285 (pounds) or so, but every week he'd have to sweat off about 10 pounds just to get to some number. Some of the stupid traditions of football were still around then."

## Tom Glassic—A Different Breed

One of the better read and engaging players in Bronco history has to be offensive lineman Tom Glassic. A long-haired, hippy-looking player out of the University of Virginia, Glassic was a mainstay of the offensive line for years and the team's pre-eminent military historian. He collected hundreds of toy soldiers, especially from the Civil War, and he had a fascination with Napoleon Bonaparte. Morton kidded him about his hair a lot, but always considered the Glass Man kind of a kindred spirit.

Glassic was a late first-round pick, but always seemed to be in a battle for his place in the NFL. He had trouble keeping his weight up, and never more so than when he got sick prior to Super Bowl XII and was offended when the Broncos drafted offensive lineman Steve Schindler with their first-round pick in 1977. But Glassic proved to be a nimble, effective blocker and he continued playing through the 1983 season.

"He was the intellectual of our team. He really was an expert on the Civil War. I went over to his place one time, and he had all these battle scenes with these little toy soldiers. He would re-create all these battle scenes, and he was smart about a lot of other military stuff, too. He was very free-spirited, in every single way. He liked to participate in a lot of the obvious things that were going on in the '70s. A lot of organic materials, let's put it that way. But what a great guy, and what an interesting guy, too. He was interested in so much more than just football, and I like guys like that."

## No Maurer, No Super Bowl

Andy Maurer, nicknamed Jumbo, was one of the lesser-publicized members of the Broncos offensive line in Morton's day. But without Maurer, Morton says, the Broncos probably never would have made it to Super Bowl XII. At least, Morton never would have finished the AFC title game against Oakland, without him.

Maurer finished up his career the following year after getting cut.

"The greatest game he ever played was that game. He was protecting my left side, and one good hit to that side of my body, and I probably was done. But he played the game of his life. He protected me perfectly, and I was able to play the game. When we got to the Super Bowl, Harvey Martin had a good day for Dallas, because he was a little quicker than Jumbo. But Martin was quicker than most offensive linemen, so it is no shame to Jumbo in what happened."

## Big J, Little G

John Grant played on the defensive line with the Broncos in the '70s, to little fanfare. Grant played 99 NFL games, from 1973 to 1979, and never made a single interception. He also played in an era when sacks were not officially compiled by NFL statisticians.

Although history might not remember Grant very well, Morton does.

"Big J, little g was a USC man, so of course I liked to give him a little bit of grief for going to such a place. But John was a guy who really made me feel at home when I came to the Broncos. We started to hang out together, and would go shoot pool a lot. We might have downed a little tequila together, but that can't be verified! He got me into a lot of situations, let's put it that way. But I loved John Grant, and he was a good family guy. He was and still is a guy with a smile always on his face. He had big, curly hair. He was our 'Larry' on the team. He would always call me and want to go to this place downtown, and the name escapes me (it might have been called the Blue Goose), but it was a time when you didn't want to go to downtown Denver. But he would always get me to go, and we'd hang out and shoot pool and have a good time, with a few cocktails. And we always got in trouble by the end of the night!"

## "Uppy"

When he retired in 1984, Rick Upchurch held or shared seven NFL punt-return records, and was a four-time Pro Bowl player. Does anybody remember that today?

Probably not many, and one of the least-acknowledged reasons of the travesty of that fact is that, as of 2008, he still was not a member of the Broncos' Ring of Fame. The unspoken reason he is not honored in that way by Pat Bowlen and the Broncos is for his admitted marijuana use, in 1983. While many in society thought Upchurch was courageous for admitting he used the illegal substance, the truth is it sequestered him to a kind of infamy with the straight-laced new owner Bowlen.

Here's the hard truth to Upchurch's moral critics: he has done more for underprivileged youth and youth in general than probably 98 percent of the population. Not long after retirement, Upchurch served as the leader of Rare Breed Sports in Pueblo, Colorado. He mentored and coached hundreds of kids in the area, including a two-year stint later as head coach of Pueblo East High School. Today, he continues to work with kids in Nevada.

As purely a football player, Upchurch was unrivaled in his time at his position. While he was officially a wide receiver, Uppy made his name and fame as a punt-return man. Bronco fans got on their feet when the opposing team got ready to kick the ball away, and he was a legitimate game-breaking threat that rival coaches had to spend extra time devising schemes to stop.

Morton doesn't remember Upchurch as just the highlight-reel, all-the-way-back return guy, though.

"He was a very good receiver, and a really, really smart football player. I tell you this with all honesty and conviction: When 'Uppy' set his mind to it, he was the most dominant player on the field, period. And let's face it, he was the greatest punt returner who

*Officially, Rick Upchurch played wide receiver, but made his name and fame as a punt-return man. When he retired in 1984, "Uppy" held or shared seven NFL punt-return records, and was a four-time Pro Bowl player.* Photo courtesy of WireImages.

ever played. Other than Bob Hayes, who I played with in Dallas, he was maybe the fastest guy of his era in the NFL. If there was anybody as fast as him when he played, I'd like to know his name. But he was more than that; Bob was kind of a sprinter turned into a football player. Uppy was a pure football player. He could really play. When he got attentive to the game, he could really play. Sometimes I think he should have played more as a receiver, because it probably would have kept his mind into the game more. When you're only returning punts, it's probably harder to do that. Of all the games I played with Uppy, the one I most remember is the comeback win (37–34) we had against Seattle (in 1979). I just remember coming into the huddle and saying 'Uppy, I need you.' And the first pass I threw, he just took it and made all these amazing moves and got us right into the game again mentally.

"Uppy today is the same person he was when he played. I love being around him. He's been so good with young kids. He's turned into a phenomenal role model, and what a credit that is when all is said and done. It's not about running back kicks and that stuff, it's about what a man you are and became, and to me there's no better example of what a man and role model should be than Uppy.

"He should at least be in the Ring of Fame, and I think he should be in the Hall of Fame, period. Who else did what he did as a punt returner?"

## Paul Smith—Mr. Smooth

Paul Smith was not a starter on the Broncos' Orange Crush defense of 1977, but he was the inspiration for just about every starter.

Smith, nicknamed Smooth, was one of the NFL's best pass rushers of the late 1960s and early '70s. He finished his career in 1978 with 55½ career sacks, but sacks were not officially kept in the NFL until 1982, so precisely how many he had might be open to debate. In any case, Smith was a dominant lineman, whose life was cut short in 2000 by pancreatic cancer.

"Paul Smith died too soon. 'Smooth' was just always relaxed, and everybody looked up to him. He was one who really started all the things when you look at the Denver defense of that era. He didn't play much when I was there, but there were so many great players ahead of him. But he never complained about anything, and he was a great leader for all those young guys coming up. I really just will always remember a guy who enjoyed himself and what he did, and just enjoyed life."

## The Egg Man

Ron Egloff played from 1977 to 1983 as a tight end with the Broncos, before finishing up his career with San Diego in '84. He played in the shadow of Riley Odoms much of his time with Denver, but made lots of big plays and was a favorite of Morton's when the going got tough.

"He was from Wisconsin, and was just a guy you could always flip the ball off to. We played a lot of double tight end formations, and he really was an important part of our team. He was a great teammate and he always kept things light in the locker room, him and Rob Lytle. Two white kids from the upper Midwest, liberal as you can be, and they just liked to talk and keep things loose."

Egloff retained some business interests in the Denver area following retirement, sharing ownership in the local bar and grill chain, Jackson's Hole.

"I saw few players in my time who liked beer as much as the Egg Man. That Wisconsin mentality, it's just ingrained in you, when it comes to drinking beer and having a good time, I think. He liked to have a good time, but he was so typical of our team in the late '70s in that, when it came time to step on the football field, they were all business. He took his job very seriously on Sunday, and so did the rest of that team. We had a lot of fun guys, but the partying stopped on Saturday night, and by Sunday morning, everybody wanted to go out and tear somebody's head off. (Running back) Jon Keyworth was another guy like the Egg Man.

Just a tough, son of a bitch who loved to play football. They didn't always play a lot, like those two, but they were all about the team and winning and those were the kinds of guys who made our team what it was. They call the '69 Mets the amazing, miracle team, but I think the '77 Broncos were kind of a miracle team in that sense. We had so many so-called no-name guys, but when you added them all up as a whole, we were a tough team to face."

## Godwin Turk—The Embalmer

When the Broncos went to New Orleans for the Super Bowl, one of the things many players did was go to the mortuary where defensive veteran Godwin Turk used to work as a younger man, growing up in New Orleans. Turk, despite his literally morbid line of work and interest, was a rib-achingly funny man who talked a mile-a-minute all with a big-time Bayou accent.

"I don't know how many dead bodies he showed those guys—and I didn't go, but I heard about it—but Godwin kept saying to us, 'The Embalmer is coming home.' He was from there, and it was exciting for him. He just talked nonstop on the way there, and it was a big deal for him."

## Joe Rizzo—The Fourth Beatle

So much was made of the Broncos' defense in 1977, with special attention given to the great linebacking corps. But, quick, can you name the four starters? Randy Gradishar, Tom Jackson, and Bob Swenson probably come to mind to many fans, but what about Joe Rizzo?

Rizzo, like Ringo of the Beatles, was the lesser-publicized and lesser-appreciated member of that great unit. But not from team-mates such as Morton.

"He was the inside middle linebacker, and he kept everything together. He allowed Gradishar, for instance, to do all the things he did. He really covered up well for him and others, the guy who did a lot of the dirty work. He was one of my favorite guys on that team. He was always there on a play. Maybe he didn't make the big tackle itself, but he did the things that allowed the big tackle to be made by another guy. I really miss him, hanging out with him. He's always one of the guys I most look forward to seeing when I go back to Denver for reunions. He was a great player for us precisely because he didn't care a lot about the publicity and all the attention. As I've said about a lot of guys on that team, they didn't care about that stuff—just winning and doing their job. They were a big influence on me, too. They really helped me develop more of that mindset as a player, when I came to Denver. I didn't care anymore about my stats and things like that after I got to Denver. The only thing I cared about was getting the win, and guys like Rizzo made a lot of those great Sunday night victory parties at the Colorado Mine Company possible."

## George Atkinson—A Bronco?

For any member of the Oakland Raiders to come and play for the Broncos in the late '70s would have seemed out of the question, and vice-versa. Many teams hated the Raiders then—and still do, as long as Al Davis is in charge—but nobody more so than the Broncos.

So, it was something of a shocker when defensive back George Atkinson signed a free-agent contract with Denver in 1979, after many years of playing what many branded a dirty, outlaw style of game for the Raiders alongside Jack Tatum. Atkinson played only six games for Denver in what would be his final NFL season, and Morton admits it took a while for Atkinson to be accepted into the Broncos locker room.

"We didn't' want any of that Raider stuff. But he really was a good guy actually. But at first you're saying to yourself, 'How the hell do you go from the Raiders to the Broncos?' You just couldn't do that. But he did a pretty nice job for us, backing up Billy

Thompson I believe, and he was fun to have around. I'm sure a lot of guys thought we got him so he could spill some secrets to us about the Raiders and their system. But that never happens. Systems change, and guys just don't do that. They might try to tell what they know, but it just never works."

## Dennis Smith—What An Athlete

One of the longest-serving players in Bronco history was a safety out of the University of Southern California, Dennis Smith.

You can make a lot of good arguments as to why Smith belongs in the Pro Football Hall of Fame, but he too, like so many other Bronco defensive players, has been overlooked. From 1981 to 1994, Smith played a fearsome brand of football for Denver. Along with Steve Atwater, Smith scared a lot of good NFL receivers from coming their way. It is something of a bitter irony for Smith, however, that he was not considered the best and biggest-hitting safety of his day. His former USC teammate, Ronnie Lott, was.

What a secondary the Trojans had in 1980; not only did Smith and Lott go on to multiple Pro-Bowl careers (Smith played in six), but the Trojans had another future NFL Pro Bowl player in the backfield, Joey Browner.

Smith was a rookie in Morton's last full year with the Broncos, and Morton still can't forget the first time he saw No. 49 on a football field.

"He could jump higher than anybody I've ever seen—anybody. It was beyond belief. Oh God, was he a great athlete, and a great player. Ronnie Lott won Super Bowls and probably got more fame than Dennis, but Dennis Smith does not take a back seat to Ronnie Lott. He was phenomenal. He was just so fast and so athletic, it blew me away. When we got him, I remember telling the defensive coaches, 'You got yourself a player for the next decade right there.' Well, he ended up playing longer than that. I had always thought we had a great defensive backfield on my earlier

Bronco teams, and then this guy comes in, and Steve Atwater later on (in 1989) and those two guys were tough to beat. Those two guys were two of the greatest that ever played, but they didn't get the recognition that they deserve."

Smith moved back to the Los Angeles area following his career, and today has a successful property management business. He was inducted into the Broncos' Ring of Fame in 2001.

## Steve DeBerg—A Kindred Spirit

Craig Morton and Steve DeBerg had a lot in common. Both played college football in Northern California. Both played nearly 20 years as a quarterback in the NFL. Both liked to work hard, and also play hard. Above all, DeBerg, like Morton, had the drive to keep working at his craft, even after things looked like they were at the end of the line. Morton remembers a player who came to

*Dubbed a "film-a-holic" by Morton for constantly watching game film, quarterback Steve DeBerg was always prepared for the opposition and ranks in the top 20 all-time for attempts, completions, and yards passing.* Photo courtesy of WireImages.

Denver, in 1981, for his eagerness—even after playing in San Francisco under Bill Walsh and Joe Montana.

"Steve was a sponge. He was always trying to learn new things. When he was traded to us, he really wanted to learn every little thing. His wife and mine were good friends, and we spent a lot of time together. He wanted to know every intricacy about playing quarterback. He wanted to know how I did every little thing, from looking off defenders to everything. He was an unbelievable student of the game. He would study films to the point where he would know the exception to every little thing. It was to the point where I got on him a little. He would be asking questions about things that might happen only 1 or 2 percent of the time, as far as a defensive scheme was concerned. But he knew what to do in that 2 percent of the time. I would always just kid him: 'Don't worry about that shit. Just worry about the main stuff. Just get the majority of what's happening, don't worry about what that one rare chance of what might happen. But he was just a film-a-holic. He just studied all the time. He later coached for Danny Reeves in New York with the Giants (and, in 1998, came out of retirement to play for Reeves with the Atlanta Falcons).

"He just kept going as a player, and that's because he really knew the game. I loved him as a teammate and I still love him. I see him maybe once or twice a year, and he's always the same guy, just a happy-go-lucky.

"There's a really funny story about me and Steve. The Raiders had a defensive lineman named Art Thoms, and every year they have a golf tournament in California, mostly with players from the Bay Area, and Steve was there as well with me one year. Art has a very gorgeous wife, and so do I, and we were all in the VIP area after our round, and my wife got up to leave the couch where she was sitting on. Steve and his wife, like I said, were great friends with me and Kym. Well, Kym left her spot, but Steve thought Art Thoms's wife was my wife all of a sudden. He came up to what he thought was Kym and gave her a big hug and kiss, but she was Art's wife. Well, Art Thoms got up and he looked at that and he slapped DeBerg and threw him off her and said 'What the hell are you doing?' Well, Steve was all apologetic and saying, 'Oh, sorry, I thought she was Kym.' Well, that story has lived for years now. He's always going to look at the blonde who hugs him. But it scared the shit out of Steve, because Art was really pissed. I've never seen a guy who had the deer-in-the-headlights look like Steve did right there. I had to step in and be the peacemaker, and everybody was laughing their asses off, except Art."

Morton could have felt threatened by DeBerg's presence when he came in 1981. After all, he passed for 3,652 yards for the 49ers in 1979. But that was a bad San Francisco team, despite names on the roster such as (rookie) Joe Montana, O.J. Simpson, Freddie Solomon, and Dwight Clark, who were coached by a man named Bill Walsh. The 49ers were 2–14, and DeBerg was shipped to the Broncos to make way for Montana.

DeBerg was expected to take Morton's starting job in '81. Morton had been in and out as a starter in the previous couple of years, but he had his best statistical season of his career. Morton might have been spurred on by DeBerg's presence, but he never held any animosity.

"I never really felt threatened by anybody about taking my job. Even Roger (Staubach). I always had enough confidence that I could play better than anybody. I knew that I always knew more than the other guys. With DeBerg, I knew that he would be a good quarterback, because he paid the price and really wanted to learn even as the backup to me. He took all the things that he learned from me and others and really had a good, long career. He was a very good, solid quarterback. And, bottom line, everybody loved DeBergie, because he was a good teammate to everybody."

## Sammy Winder—Tough S.O.B.

Morton's last season in the NFL, 1982, was Sammy Winder's first.

They only played two games together, but Winder made a strong impression on the 39-year-old quarterback.

"He was a tough son of a bitch. I loved playing with him. He was just your typical Bronco: just a good, good guy. It just seemed like we always had those kinds of guys in Denver. You didn't have those pain-in-the-ass kinds of guys. Sammy would run the football as hard as you can run it, and had a great attitude."

Winder is probably one of the lesser-appreciated Bronco players from his era, 1982–90. He played in two Pro Bowls and led the team in rushing from 1983 to 1987, including a career-high 1,153 in 1984. Despite that, he has not been included in the Broncos' Ring of Fame. He was known for his "Mississippi Mud Walk" dance after he scored a touchdown. Winder was an excellent AFC post-season performer, running for 102 yards in a 1986 divisional playoff win at home against New England, and 83 yards the next week in the The Drive game in Cleveland.

The only games that didn't go well in the postseason, nor for the team as a whole, were the three Super Bowls he played. He only ran the ball 13 times in those games, for a net 25 yards.

## Rick Parros—The Handsome One

Quick, name the Broncos' leading rusher in 1981? If you had trouble naming the correct answer, Rick Parros, you're not alone.

Parros ran for 749 yards on 176 carries, a solid 4.3 average. But like many Bronco teams of mid-'70s on to the '90s, the running game took a backstage role to the defense and the quarterback.

That '81 season would be the best of Parros' short career. With his curly hair and boyish looks, he was a hit with the ladies and a target for needlers such as Morton.

"He was the handsome one. We gave him a hard time over his hair. But he was just the sweetest, nicest guy and a very good player. He had a real good year for us in '81 and made a lot of big runs in clutch situations."

## The Sarge

Dave Preston played in the backfield with the Broncos from 1978 to 1983 and, again, to little fanfare. He was just another tough, grinding runner, good in the trenches but not a breakaway threat.

Preston was a very good receiver for a running back, catching 52 passes in '81, for a 9.8-yard average. He was a favorite of Morton in check down situations, and on third down.

"He was the best third-down receiver out of the backfield, for sure. The Sarge was tough. He had these huge legs, and was very tough to bring down. And, I've said this before, but he was one of the great teammates. I keep saying the same thing about all these guys, but Dave was just the best. And the fans loved him. He was just a great role player, a guy you could always count on. He was never hurt, and you could always just count on him being in the huddle."

## Norris Weese—Gone Too Soon

Norris Weese, who played backup to Morton primarily with the Broncos, died in 1995 of bone cancer.

It was a life cut far too short. In Weese's final days, he received a visitor to his Georgia hospital bed: Morton.

"He just kept fighting, even though he had all these rods in him and things, and on all kinds of medicine. The last conversation I had with him, we both cried so hard. We knew it would be the last time we saw each other. Two days later, he died. He was a good man. He was my chief competitor for the starting job with the Broncos. Craig Penrose probably had more talent, but Norris just had that bulldog-type of mentality to him, and he was going to do something spectacular no matter what. So, I always respected him. His family lived right near mine in Denver, so we were always visiting together, as we did with a lot of players' families, because we all lived in the same area."

# chapter 5
# Authority Figures

*"Joe taught me more about the game than anybody. He really was the architect and the brains behind that Orange Crush defense. He just was so smart, and not just about football. He probably could have been at NASA or some place like that. But I'm glad he decided to teach football, because he made my career and a lot of others a lot better."*

—Broncos cornerback Billy Thompson

The Broncos have had remarkable stability in management since the early 1980s. Pat Bowlen has owned the team since 1984, and the Broncos have had only three head coaches in that time, entering 2008. There were other notable assistants, some of whom are detailed here.

## Pat Bowlen—No Better Owner

Craig Morton never played for a Broncos team owned by Pat Bowlen, but he wastes little time in calling Bowlen the best owner in the NFL. No doubt that is partly because of Bowlen's reputation for treating Broncos alumni very well, including paid transportation for many players and wives to come back to Denver for various events. Bowlen instituted the Broncos' Ring of Fame, of which Morton is a member.

Bowlen, whose father, Paul, became a millionaire in the Western Canadian oil business, rubbed a lot of people the wrong way in his early years. He memorably wore a fur coat on the sidelines on cold days, and seemed to have a permanent sneer on his face.

The truth is Bowlen did have an arrogance to him, but it can't be denied that he did a lot of good things for people, and not just for current and past players. He was very active in charity work, including serving as the director of the Colorado Special Olympics for years.

"Pat Bowlen does absolutely everything in a first-class way. Every time I come back for anything, he just makes everything so easy, and he does that for every player, not just me. He really cares about the history of the Broncos, and the guys who helped build the franchise to what it is today. A lot of owners, they get a team and don't know a damn thing about what happened before. Not him. Guys really, really appreciate that. Really, he doesn't owe any of us a damn thing, but he really goes all out for alumni—and he does a lot of things for guys that don't get any publicity at all. To me, I think he's the model NFL owner, and you look at a lot of the success that franchise has had since he took over, and it's no accident.

"And the thing is, he doesn't seek a lot of headlines for himself like so many other owners do. When's the last time you read a headline where Pat Bowlen is spouting off about some thing, or making some kind of jackass controversial statement? It doesn't happen. He just gets good people under him and lets them do their job, and doesn't try to insert himself in all kinds of things that they were hired to do."

"I second what Craig says," kicker Jim Turner says. "Pat Bowlen is the best owner in sports."

## Mike Shanahan—From Quarterback Coach To Face of Franchise

Craig Morton's successor as Broncos quarterbacks coach in 1989 was, technically, not Mike Shanahan. But, in practical terms, he was.

Shanahan was fired as head coach of the Los Angeles Raiders in '89, after a 1–3 start. He posted a 7–9 record in his only full season at the L.A. helm the year before. From 1985 to 1987, Shanahan was the Broncos' offensive coordinator for Dan Reeves, so he looked to the Broncos again when he was put out of work by Raiders' owner Al Davis.

The Broncos obliged, but this time made him just the quarterbacks coach, as Chan Gailey was the offensive coordinator. What was perceived as a steep career setback at the time might have been the best thing that ever happened to Shanahan.

He developed a closer one-on-one relationship with John Elway, who feuded often with Reeves. Shanahan became a better sounding board to Elway than Morton, who was, truth be told, much more loyal to Reeves as a friend than to Elway.

Despite the Broncos having a 5–11 record in 1990, Shanahan was elevated back to the job of offensive coordinator, and Denver posted a 12–4 record in '91. Just as Elway was coming to love life

*Mike Shanahan first worked as the Broncos quarterback coach and developed a close relationship with superstar quarterback John Elway. Shanahan left and returned to the Broncos as head coach in 1995, leading them to back-to-back Super Bowl victories.*

with Shanahan again, the coach was lured away by the powerhouse San Francisco 49ers to serve in the same capacity.

San Francisco won one Super Bowl and went to two NFC Championship Games in Shanahan's three years. In 1995, he landed his second NFL head-coaching job with the Broncos.

Entering 2008, Shanahan was still on the job. Despite only one playoff victory following Elway's retirement, he seemed firmly in control and in owner Pat Bowlen's good graces.

Shanahan was your typical, Type-A football man, a lifer. At the tender age of 23, he was an assistant coach for the University of Oklahoma, for a 1975 team that won the national championship. He then went on to coach at schools such as Northern Arizona, Eastern Illinois, Minnesota, and the University of Florida, before entering the NFL for good in 1984 as the Broncos' receivers coach.

Shanahan was crowned as NFL royalty for being the head man when the Broncos won their back-to-back Super Bowls in the late '90s, but some have been critical of his work since losing Elway, especially several of his free-agent signings and trades. Cornerback Dale Carter was one notable bust, as were several defensive linemen acquired from the Cleveland Browns in the mid-2000s. He also wasted a third-round draft choice in 2005 on star-crossed running back Maurice Clarett, who was cut not long afterward.

Still, Shanahan's overall time with the Broncos has to be considered a success. Entering the '08 season, Shanahan had the second-longest tenure of any NFL head coach, behind Tennessee's Jeff Fisher.

He is considered to have one of the better offensive minds in NFL history, helping the 49ers better develop the "West Coast" offense first put into practice by Bill Walsh. He also had a knack for churning out consistently good running backs, with Denver regularly having top performers such as Terrell Davis, Clinton Portis, Mike Anderson, Cleveland Gary, Tatum Bell, and Reuben Droughns.

But some wonder if he wasn't beginning to suffer from burnout after a bad 2007 season (7–9 record, Denver's worst since 1999). Included was an embarrassing 41–3 home loss to the San Diego Chargers in week 5, and an even more unsightly 44–7 drubbing at the hands of mediocre Detroit on November 4th.

Not so, said Shanahan. He said he retained as much fervor for the job as the day he was hired, and believed he had a star of the future in young quarterback Jay Cutler, a first-round pick from Vanderbilt.

## Bill Belichick—The Gofer

There is no question as to which NFL coach commands the most respect, fear, admiration and mystique in today's game: Bill Belichick of the New England Patriots.

He wasn't always that way, of course, but few people realize he got part of his start in the NFL with the 1978 Broncos—in a most unglamorous way. Morton remembers his team's former assistant special teams and defensive assistant coach as a quiet "gofer" to head coach Red Miller.

"Red Miller hired him, because his father and Red were very close friends. But Belichick then was this guy that was the all-time gofer. He did everything that was the most unpleasant thing to do. When we'd be out practicing sometimes in freezing temperatures, he would be the guy in the tower taking the film. He would do all the jobs that nobody else wanted to do, and he never complained. You never knew what he was thinking about, because he didn't say much. But he would just do everything, and you could think even back then that there was something amazing about the guy. We'd all, as players, get back to the locker room and be complaining our asses off about the cold and then he walks in and he's got icicles out of his nose. And he never said a word of complaint, and he did it every single day. The things that he's achieved, I'm not all that surprised. He is deserving, because the fact is he worked his ass off to get where he is, and nobody started lower than him."

## Joe Collier: The Professor

Joe Collier is considered one of the great football coaches of all time. That he was an assistant most of his long pro career doesn't matter to the players who played for him. Collier was a great coach, period. Morton remembers a very smart man who not only knew numbers and every football theory there was, but also someone who knew how to relate to people.

"He was like the physicist. He knew so much about science and just so many other things. But as smart as he was, a lot smarter than most of us dummy players, guys just loved him and loved playing for him. He treated you like a man. Guys just respected the hell out of him, and he was one of the really great defensive coaches in the history of the league. He was the man behind the curtain of our great defenses."

Collier was a head coach with Buffalo of the AFL from 1966 to 1968 before joining Denver as an assistant to Lou Saban in 1969. An all-Big Ten selection as an end at Northwestern, Collier was drafted by the New York Giants, but enlisted in the Army instead of trying for a pro playing career. He is credited with perfecting the 3–4 defense, which relied on four quick linebackers for total effectiveness. Collier certainly had that in 1977, with Tom Jackson, Randy Gradishar, Bob Swenson, and Joe Rizzo.

Longtime Broncos cornerback Billy Thompson, a Ring of Fame member, calls Collier the smartest man he ever knew in football.

"Joe taught me more about the game than anybody. He really was the architect and the brains behind that Orange Crush defense. He just was so smart, and not just about football. He probably could have been at NASA or some place like that. But I'm glad he decided to teach football, because he made my career and a lot of others a lot better."

## Jerry Frei: A Good Egg

The Broncos' offensive line coach in 1981 and '82 was Jerry Frei, a former World War II fighter pilot who flew 67 combat missions in the Pacific theater. As we've seen, Morton's father had a lot in common with men such as Jerry Frei.

Frei was the head coach of the Oregon Ducks for five years in the 1960s and early '70s, coaching players such as Ahmad Rashad and Dan Fouts. He played college ball at Wisconsin, with teammates such as All-Americans Dave Schreiner and Elroy "Crazylegs" Hirsch.

Frei, like many WWII vets, never talked about his war experiences. Morton never heard any of his father's stories from New Guinea, and he never heard any from Frei, either. The only thing Frei wanted to talk about was winning football strategy, although Morton always figured Frei had been through some kind of physical hell.

"He was a great guy, with a very good disposition all the time. But you could always sense that he was in a lot of pain. I don't know if it was more from the war or from football, but you could tell he was really always suffering from injuries. (Frei's son, Terry, a longtime Denver sports writer and author, says his dad actually suffered his worst injuries playing softball for a barnstorming team). He had a really pronounced limp and he just always looked like he was having a hard time. But you never heard him complain about a single thing. He was just one of those guys who worked hard and didn't complain, and that was that. He just had that inner strength that so many guys who served in the war and lived to come back had. Kids of guys like that, like me, didn't know what they went through until we ourselves got older. But guys like Jerry Frei and my dad are the ones who risked their lives to keep our country great—and free.

"You knew Jerry Frei was a good egg, because his linemen loved him. When you see linemen who love their offensive line coach, you know that guy is a good guy."

## Kaiser's Plane

Edgar Kaiser had a brief tenure as Broncos owner in the early 1980s, but Morton has good memories of playing for him. One of the Morton's peculiar memories of Kaiser, however, was of his travel arrangements.

"He wouldn't fly on the team plane, but he would fly at the same time as us, on his own private jet, a G-4 or something. We'd take off at the same time, but he would be right next to us in his own plane. He always had business other places, I guess, so he had to get away fast. But he would always be there at the airport, welcoming us after we had just landed. He was just always a little eccentric that way, flying with his own little group of people. But he really loved owning the Broncos. He really reveled in it. And, of course, the best thing he ever did for the team was getting John Elway from the Colts. He's the one who engineered that whole deal, and a lot of people have forgotten that."

# chapter 6
# The Broncos, Pre- and Post-Morton

*"How we ever won a game playing in those uniforms, I guess I'll never know. You felt embarrassed putting them on. They called the jerseys we wore mustard color. I called them puke yellow. The socks made you feel like a clown. Maybe those first few games, we just scared teams to death."*

—Frank Tripucka,
the Broncos' first quarterback

## In The Beginning...

The Denver Broncos were born in 1960, part of a group of eight teams that decided to call themselves the American Football League. Seen as an inferior, shabby, loathsome entity by the established NFL, the AFL nonetheless plowed ahead, playing in mostly second-rate stadiums.

Most people don't realize the Broncos' first owners, the Howsam family from Denver, did not have football as their first sporting love. In 1947, Bob, Lee, and Earl Howsam bought the Denver Bears, a minor-league baseball team in the old Western League, for $75,000. What the Howsams most dreamed of was to eventually lure a Major League Baseball team to Denver, but they could never break through all the red tape and financial difficulties to get one.

By 1960, the Howsams thought a pro football team, even filled by players called "NFL rejects" by the media, might make the city of Denver seem more big-time to a potential MLB team. Bob Howsam would leave Denver to become the general manager of baseball's St. Louis Cardinals and later the Cincinnati Reds during their "Big Red Machine" days of the 1970s.

Those first Broncos teams, it is easy to see, were shabbily dressed and financed. Players wore brown pants, white belts, and ridiculous looking vertically striped socks—hand-me-down uniforms from a college football all-star game. They wore those same uniforms for home and road games. There was little hype before their first game. In fact, three days before their first game, the headline in *The Denver Post* sports section was "Broncos Drill For Loop Debut." This game between Denver and the Boston Patriots on September 9, 1960, was the first in AFL history.

Clearly, Broncomania was a long ways off.

"We played our first three games on the road. We won the first two, and should have won the third," said Frank Tripucka, the team's first quarterback. "And we won our first game back at home. How we ever won a game playing in those uniforms, I guess I'll never know. You felt embarrassed putting them on. They called the jerseys we wore mustard color. I called them puke yellow. The socks made you feel like a clown. Maybe those first few games, we just scared teams to death. But we still played hard as a team, and I look back on those first Broncos teams with pride. We didn't win a lot, but we tried to give the fans a good effort for their money, and we had some pretty high-scoring games."

The 3–1 start seemed almost miraculous, considering the Broncos were 0–5 in the pre-season, including a 43–6 loss to Boston. But the team won only one more game the rest of the season, and the franchise would not have its first winning season until 1973.

There was lots of bad football in Denver those first 13 seasons.

"The problem Denver had was, they just didn't have very good athletes. They just had a lot of guys that were not in very good shape," said former Broncos kicker Jim Turner, who played in the AFL with the New York Jets before being traded to Denver in 1971, two years after winning the Super Bowl with Joe Namath and company. "My first couple years with the Broncos, we just didn't have the athletes on the field to compete. And, it was just a losing attitude. Guys accepted losing. As long as we put up a good fight for a quarter or a half, guys would walk out of the locker room satisfied after a game we lost. It took a while for a new mindset to sink in with the Broncos. It was really tough for a while."

The Broncos had a lot of bad quarterbacks, especially after Tripucka retired in 1963. Forgettable quarterbacks such as Jackie Lee, Mickey Slaughter, Max Choboian, Steve Tensi, Pete Liske, Don Horn, and Steve Ramsey populated the Denver backfield in those years, all spectacularly unsuccessfully.

Tensi was so unpopular in Denver that he received death threats from an alleged Bronco fan. The threat came from a man—still unidentified—who said he would shoot Tensi from the Holiday Inn, a circularly-constructed hotel that overlooked Mile High Stadium. Security was tight, and thankfully nothing happened.

The Broncos did have the first black quarterback, Marlin Briscoe, in 1968. Briscoe had some excellent games, but head coach Lou Saban never quite believed in him as a quarterback, and he was traded to Buffalo the following season and was converted to a receiver. Briscoe still harbors some ill will toward Saban for never giving him more of a chance to prove himself as a quarterback.

"When I look back on my football career, I still think of myself as a quarterback," said Briscoe, who went on to win two Super Bowl rings with the Miami Dolphins as a receiver. "I really think that if I'd gotten that chance, we could have become a real good team, with me as a quarterback. But Lou just didn't think I was cut out to be the guy, and he wanted Steve Tensi. He must have wanted him, because he gave up two first-round draft picks for him!"

The Broncos never had a starting quarterback complete more than 55 percent of his passes until 1972, when veteran Charley Johnson was obtained from Houston. Johnson got Denver its first winning season, 7–5–2, in '73, and became enshrined in the Broncos' Ring of Fame. Johnson in many ways was a quarterback similar to Morton, an older, gunslinger type with not a lot of mobility. He was a veteran of 11 NFL seasons, mostly with St. Louis, when he came to Denver. Like Morton, he would enjoy some of the best years of his career in his final few as a Bronco.

Today Johnson is a professor of chemical engineering at New Mexico State, quite a career change for a quarterback.

Ramsey succeeded Johnson as the starter in 1975, and many predicted stardom for the former North Texas standout. But, despite leading the Broncos to a 9–5 season in 1976, Ramsey was a liability on too many Sundays. He threw more interceptions (13) than touchdowns (11) and completed only 47.4 percent of his passes. Ramsey was slow with his decisions at times in the pocket and was prone to throwing the ball in high-traffic areas.

The New York Giants thought Ramsey still had potential when they acquired him after the '76 season, giving up Morton in return. But Ramsey never played a game with the Giants. He was cut by the team and retired from the NFL, losing the starting job to Joe Pisarcik.

"When I came to the Broncos from the Giants, people thought I would be just another unsuccessful Denver quarterback," Morton said. "I knew the team had never had a really top quarterback, although I think Charley Johnson was a really excellent quarter-back and did a lot of good things with Denver. But I was well aware of the team's reputation, of Denver being a place where quarterbacks went to die. I certainly didn't want that to happen with me, but that's pretty much what everyone thought would happen. It was nice to prove them wrong."

## The Half-A-Loaf Game

The 1970 Denver Broncos started the season 3–0, but finished 5–8–1. In the first game of the following season, coach Lou Saban had to open the season against a powerfully good Miami Dolphins team at Mile High Stadium.

He had a chance, a good chance, to open the year 1–0, but opted not to try for a game-winning field goal at the end. Instead, Saban opted to take a 10–10 tie. But the fallout of his conser-vatism forever soured him to Bronco fans, and Saban didn't help himself with a post-game quote concerning bread.

The Broncos had the ball with 1:14 left in regulation, tied 10–10, in good field position. Saban called three straight running plays to Floyd Little, who got a first down, but the plays used up a lot of time. Saban finally called a pass play, and netted 12 yards on a screen from quarterback Don Horn. But a holding penalty pushed the ball back, a little out of new kicker Jim Turner's range. Still, 15 seconds remained on the clock. Plenty of time for another sideline pass and send in Turner for the winning kick.

Instead, Saban called for Little to run the ball, and the tired star was hit at the line of scrimmage and, with no timeouts, the Broncos saw the clock expire. Where were the guts? Where was the winning desire?

After the game, Saban tried to rationalize his play calling to the Denver sports writers, saying: "It's an old saying, but I'd rather have half a loaf than none."

Bronco players took Saban's decision-making as a no-confidence vote, and it immediately sunk morale. The team lost the next three games, two of them at home. Fans began throwing literal half loaves of bread at Saban, including some onto the lawn of his Denver home.

With his team's record at 2–6–1, Saban resigned, with that '1' at the end of the record being the albatross that sunk his Bronco career.

"I remember just standing on the sideline, getting ready to get a chance to go on the field for a kick," Turner said. "When it didn't happen, when we didn't go for it, I was just like, 'What?' No question, it hurt our morale, and that was the kind of thing that always seemed to weigh us down as a team those years in the early '70s."

## Floyd Little: Fired, Then Re-hired

Running back Little was probably the Broncos' first big star player, although wide receiver Lionel Taylor was superb for some bad Broncos early teams.

As longtime Bronco cornerback Billy Thompson put it: "Our whole offense was Floyd right, Floyd left."

Little was beloved by the Bronco faithful, but not always by Saban. In fact, on November 24, 1968, Little was fired from the team late in the game—only to be the hero in the end.

With the Broncos leading 31–29 with two minutes left against the Buffalo Bills, Little fumbled the ball away. Buffalo quickly capitalized with a field goal for a 32–31 lead. Saban, so incensed over the fumble, told Little to "Get the hell out of here, you're fired. Highway 25 runs north and south, 70 east and west. Take your pick out of town."

A little background here: Saban was the former head coach of the Bills, and there was no team he wanted to beat more on this day than them. Saban coached the Bills to back-to-back AFL championships, but quit the team in 1965 to coach the Maryland Terps. He came back to the AFL with the Broncos in '67.

Little's fumble, which occurred after he stumbled on a rough patch of Mile High Stadium turf, would now cost Saban his cherished victory.

Stunned, Little initially walked up the runway tunnel out of the stadium. But halfway through, he thought, "Screw that" and came running back out on the field. No way was Lou Saban going to run him out of the AFL and the Denver Broncos, Little told himself.

Little rejoined the Bronco huddle after they got the ball back, on their own 31 with 25 seconds left. Saban was still screaming at Little to get off the field. Fran Lynch was in the game as Little's replacement, and if the Broncos didn't act quickly, they would get a too-many-men-on-the-field penalty.

A game of chicken ensued, with Little refusing to get off the field, against Saban's orders. Finally, Lynch threw his hands in the air in confusion and ran off the field. Knowing there wasn't much Saban could do now, Little told his quarterback, Marlin Briscoe, to air out a pass to him. He would catch it, Little promised, as along as he got the ball anywhere near him.

That's just what happened. Little ran a fly pattern and caught a 59-yard strike from Briscoe. One play later, Bobby Howfield kicked the winning field goal, and Bronco players joyfully threw their helmets in the air. Everybody except Little, who was still so stung by Saban's rebuke that he sat on the bench and wept, his face in his hands.

Despite an All-American career at Syracuse and already considered a rising young AFL star, Little was an ultra-sensitive man with fierce pride. Saban hurt him to the core, and it was his turn to tell off Saban in a most profane way when the coach approached him in reconciliation.

After a few more choice words and tense moments, Little finally bucked up a little and Saban told him, "You've got one more week."

Nearly 30 years later, Little recounted his overall memories of Saban, for orangeandblueblog.com:

"I loved playing for Lou Saban. It took a while for me to realize that we were a lot alike. We were both very intense competitors who hated to lose. I thought Lou made some great decisions, especially trading for Rich Jackson in 1967, who, at the time was a backup linebacker for the Raiders. He also drafted Billy Thompson from a small school, one of the greatest Broncos ever. I understand he got rid of Curley Culp, but who knew he would become a good player? He was only with the club for one year and he didn't start. So Lou traded him to Kansas City for something like a 3rd-or-4th-round draft pick that turned out to be guard Mike Schnitker, a local guy from Colorado who was pretty good. The questionable trades were when he tried to find quarterbacks. The Steve Tensi trade with San Diego was the biggest flop. He gave up our first round picks in 1968 and '69 for Steve and he was only a backup.

"Steve had it pretty rough during his short career in Denver. He was a tall, gutsy quarterback but everyone realized pretty quickly that he wasn't worth those two first-rounders. The fans never let him forget it either. Unfortunately, he even endured a few death threats. One of them was from a deranged person who threatened to shoot him during a game from atop of the Holiday Inn that overlooked Mile High Stadium. None of us would stand near him during pre-game stretching or the national anthem. Nothing ever came from it, but no one wanted to be struck by some stray bullet!"

Little also talked about the Broncos' later history as a factory for running backs, and comparing his era to theirs.

"It's difficult for me to compare with today's players, because I played during a time when the rules didn't benefit the offense. To the contrary, the defense held the advantage. They were allowed to clothesline you, grab you around the neck and head, and hold you up so another player could take a shot at you. I think if I played now behind the Broncos zone-blocking scheme my numbers would be off the charts. We didn't have the talent on offense that today's Broncos have, but my teammates had tremendous passion for the game. Most were not Pro Bowl players, but they busted their butts on every play. I think just having another huge weapon like John Elway would have taken a lot of the pressure off me."

## "The Drive"

Craig Morton still calls it "the best drive I've ever seen."

It happened on January 11, 1987, at Cleveland Stadium, on a wind-whipped, cold and grey day. It was the AFC Championship Game, between the visiting Broncos and Cleveland Browns. The winner would get a ticket to Pasadena, Calif., for the Super Bowl.

With five minutes, 43 seconds left in regulation, it appeared that team would be the Browns. They had a 20–13 lead on Denver, after receiver Brian Brennan caught a 48-yard touchdown bomb from quarterback Bernie Kosar.

Coached by Marty Schottenheimer, the Browns had a hard-hitting defense and had been holding quarterback John Elway

*With just five minutes left in the game, quarterback John Elway and the Broncos pull off a 15-play drive and "low-heater" 5-yard pass to win the AFC Championship against the Cleveland Browns, 23–20.*
Photo courtesy of AP Images.

pretty well in check to that point. On the ensuing kickoff, Browns veteran Mark Moseley kicked short. The ball hit the frozen turf at the 15-yard line and skidded past Broncos return man Ken Bell.

Bell hustled back and picked up the ball, only to be swarmed. The Broncos had a first-and-10 at their own 2. Only 98 yards to go for a tie.

"We got 'em right where we want 'em," Broncos offensive lineman Keith Bishop told his cold, backed-up teammates in the huddle.

Players always say stuff like that in times of desperation. Rarely does any of it come to fruition. But those teams never had a player like John Elway.

Elway would lead the Broncos on a 15-play, game-tying drive, culminating with his "low heater" 5-yard pass to Mark Jackson with 42 seconds left. Probably the biggest play of the drive was a 20-yard pass to Jackson on a third-and-18 from the Cleveland 48. Elway was sacked for an eight-yard loss on the play before, and Cleveland's notorious Dawg Pound section of fans was woofing and throwing literal dog biscuits onto the field.

"They were not just those little dog bones, either," Broncos kicker Rich Karlis said. "They were the big ones, and they hurt if they hit you."

Before the 20-yarder to Jackson, the snap from center Billy Bryan to Elway, in the shotgun, hit wide receiver Steve Watson, who was crossing in motion. The ball grazed Watson's left hip, causing Elway to reach down and lose his vision downfield. The Browns got a good pass rush and appeared to have him for another sack. But Elway sidestepped the pressure and found Jackson.

Other than Fran Tarkenton, Elway might have been the best ever at making something out of a busted play.

On the tying pass, a play called Option Left 62 Rebel, Elway threw the ball so hard that Jackson said he felt like he'd been, "hit in the chest with a cannonball." But it wasn't too hard that Jackson couldn't hang on, and The Drive was complete.

What a lot of people fail to remember was: that wasn't the end of the game.

"They got the ball to start the overtime!" Karlis says. "They won the coin toss, and I'd be lying if we weren't a little worried the drive would go for nothing. They had just scored before that, don't forget, and Kosar was a good quarterback."

Schottenheimer, who would be tortured by Elway his entire career, gathered his team together to start the overtime and proclaimed: "This is the Browns' period."

Not quite. The Browns got the ball in decent field position, at their own 30, but the fired-up Bronco defense forced a three-and-out series. Broncos lineman Karl Mecklenburg and Rulon Jones stopped Browns running back Herman Fontenot on third-and-2 to send the Cleveland punting unit on the field.

That's when the Dawg Pound started to get very, very quiet. "You could sense it," Karlis said. "They were scared to death of Elway by that point, as they should have been."

Elway got the ball at his own 25, not great normally, but paradise compared to the last drive. He soon would hit tight end Orson Mobley with a 20-yard pass to the Cleveland 48, but faced another tough third-and-12 situation, but found Watson after a scramble to get the ball to the Browns 22. Three plays later, at the Cleveland 16, Karlis and his bare right foot jogged onto the field.

"It's just like practice, it's just like practice!" Elway yelled at Karlis, for encouragement.

Yup, just like practice: freezing conditions, dog biscuits everywhere, grown men woofing through rubber dog masks—all with a trip to the Super Bowl on the line.

"I kind of glanced at John and said, 'Yeah, right,'" Karlis said. "I was mainly just concerned with getting good footing on the kick and clearing the dog bones away."

Elway was too nervous to look. So was Watson. Elway was mad he hadn't gotten the ball closer than the 16. A 33-yard field goal is short for an NFL kicker, but no chip shot, especially in those conditions.

When Karlis first struck the ball, it looked wide left. As it floated high toward the goal post, it was going to be close. Goal posts were not as high then as they are today, and the ball ascended over the post as it crossed its bisection. Referees wasted little time: good!

"We're going to the Super Bowl, boys," Broncos linebacker Jim Ryan told Elway and Watson, looking down at the ground as the kick was made.

The Broncos were going back to the Super Bowl for the first time since Morton's '77 team, and nobody was happier than the old No. 7.

"What an unbelievable job Elway did on that tying drive. To go the length of the football field, against a fired-up defense just a few minutes from going to a Super Bowl, on their home field, in front of those fans—I mean, wow. If you watch that whole drive, it's unbelievable, the command he had. That is such a tough thing, getting out of a field-position hole like that. I remember when we won that game, a feeling of pride that I'm sure came over a lot of the guys from the '77 team. Some of the guys from that '77 team were on that team, too, guys like Billy Bryan and Tom Jackson. I'm sure it was a great feeling to get back to another Super Bowl, that far apart. That doesn't happen very often. The Super Bowl didn't end the way we wanted again, but that win in Cleveland was just a great, great accomplishment."

## The Super Bowl Blowouts

The Broncos went to three more Super Bowls in the eight years after Morton's retirement. But they all ended in even bigger blowouts than Morton's one in orange and blue.

The Broncos lost to the Giants, Redskins, and 49ers, the latter an embarrassing 55–10 defeat in New Orleans in 1990. The 49ers became the first NFL team to score two touchdowns in each quarter, while John Elway was 10–for-26 for 108 yards and two interceptions. The former Golden Boy was now seen nationally as football's Ernie Banks, the guy who couldn't win the big one.

Denver, like Minnesota and (later) Buffalo, was the city of chokers, 0–4 in the sport's biggest game. The first three losses, while tough to stomach, still left a feeling of goodwill among Bronco fans, with a "we'll get 'em next year" sentiment. But by 1990, and after the biggest blowout in Super Bowl history at their expense, Bronco fans just became fed up. Now, there was anger.

Woody Paige, writing for *The Denver Post*, summed it up: "Elvis is still not alive, and neither were the Denver Broncos yesterday. In comparison, the Falklands War was closer. The troops at the Alamo held out longer. Voltaire accurately described this game hundreds of years ago: 'They squeezed the orange and threw away the skins.'"

The one loss that still makes a few Bronco players shake their heads is Super Bowl XXII, January 31, 1988, to the Redskins at Jack Murphy Stadium in San Diego.

So many things, when added up, made Bronco fans believe this was their year to win it all. Namely, they had learned what it took to win from losing to the Giants the year before. They were a solid 10–4–1 in 1987, with Elway throwing for 3,198 yards in a more wide-open offense better tailored to his talents. They were hungrier, more mature and up against a Washington team that only had the third-best record in the NFC and struggled some in winning their conference playoff games.

At no point were Bronco fans more convinced it was their time than after the first quarter. Their team had a 10–0 lead, partly from a 56-yard touchdown pass from Elway to Ricky Nattiel on the game's first play.

And then it all went to Hell.

The Redskins, behind veteran quarterback Doug Williams, who had struggled in the playoffs, scored 35 points in the second quarter. THIRTY-FIVE POINTS IN THE SECOND QUARTER. Final score: Washington 42, Denver 10. Lots of people who were there still don't know what happened.

"Nobody could understand," kicker Rich Karlis said. "That was a truly bad place to be, our locker room at halftime. You looked up at the scoreboard, 35–10, and it just didn't seem possible. We just couldn't get ourselves back in the game mentally from there."

Morton watched the game, and would soon be coaching the Broncos at the behest of Reeves.

"That might have been the most bizarre football game I ever saw," Morton said. "Washington just kept scoring and scoring and scoring in the second quarter, and you couldn't believe the score when you finally looked up. I know how things can get away from you quickly in a game like that, though. Your mistakes become magnified in that game. Things can snowball quickly. But I don't think I've ever seen a game swing so far, so fast, like that one."

The loss to the Giants in Super Bowl XXI was also tough to swallow, as the Broncos had the lead in that one as well. But things started to go south when Karlis missed a chip-shot field goal at the end of the first half that would have made it 13–7 instead of an eventual 10–9.

The Giants used the missed 23-yarder by Karlis and a late first-half safety on Elway as momentum toward a dominant second half. Giants quarterback Phil Simms was an incredible 22-for-25 passing in what would be the game of his life. When he hit Phil McConkey with a deflected touchdown pass to start the fourth quarter, the score was 33–10.

The mystifying, disappointing thing about all four of the Broncos' first Super Bowl losses was how poorly their defense played. Granted, they faced some of the game's great quarter-backs in players Roger Staubach and Joe Montana. But just how thoroughly the Denver defense was steamrolled in large parts of each game hurt the Orange Crush legacy some. Simms and Williams were both very good quarterbacks, but they looked like a combination of Montana, Staubach, and Johnny Unitas when they played Denver in the big one.

"Those losses hurt the fans a lot," Morton said. "But it's still a hell of an accomplishment to get to a Super Bowl, and the fact that we did it three times in 10 years, after our first trip, says a lot. But that's the nature of the beast; it's a great ride in getting there, but losing it makes it feel like the end of the world, that none of it mattered."

## Broncos Finally Win It All—And Morton Was There

Only the hardest of hard-core Broncomaniacs probably know that Craig Morton was on the field the night the Broncos finally won their first Super Bowl, in 1998, against Green Bay in San Diego.

Morton was hired by a Denver TV station at the time (Ch. 4) to do some commentary, and wasn't standing too far away from John Elway, as the Duke of Denver jumped in the air when linebacker John Mobley knocked down Brett Favre's last pass to wrap up the win. Morton threw a fist in the air as well, and still talks about the win as a "we," not "they."

What a game it was. The Broncos came in as underdogs to the defending champion Packers, and gave up a touchdown on the Packers' third play from scrimmage, a Brett Favre pass to Antonio Freeman.

"Here we go again," everybody who bled orange and blue thought. Another Super Bowl blowout loss, followed by another Blue Monday. But this Denver team truly was different. For starters, it finally had a big-time, game-breaking running back in Terrell Davis.

Davis was named the MVP of the 31–24 victory, and he didn't even play in the second quarter, except for one play as a decoy. Davis forgot to take medicine as a precaution against the frequent migraine headaches he suffered, and, sure enough, a migraine developed in earnest after he was kicked in the helmet on an early play.

Thanks to the longer halftime of the Super Bowl, Davis was mostly pain-free by the start of the third quarter. He proceeded to create a lot of pain for the Packers' defensive line, finishing with 157 yards and three touchdown runs.

The Packers' Eugene Robinson, who would be arrested for soliciting a prostitute as an Atlanta Falcon the night before the Super Bowl the next year, tried to fire up teammates by comparing the Broncos to the awful Indianapolis Colts. It didn't work. The Broncos were simply a more talented team than any of the first

*John Elway, the "Duke of Denver" jumps in the air when linebacker John Mobley knocked down Brett Favre's last pass to wrap up the Super Bowl XXXII win. The Broncos became just the second wild card team to win the Super Bowl.* Photo courtesy of AP Images.

four that lost Super Bowls, especially offensively, largely because of Davis.

The Broncos' road to San Diego was termed the Revenge Tour. They started the postseason with a huge payback victory at home over Jacksonville, 42–17. Then came road victories at Kansas City and Pittsburgh. Against the favored Steelers, Denver pulled out a 24–21 victory, thanks to multiple interceptions of former University of Colorado quarterback Kordell Stewart, and a clutch third-down, one-armed catch by Shannon Sharpe to effectively run out of the clock.

The two weeks leading up to the Super Bowl were predictably filled with many stories about Denver's past futility. No AFC team had won a championship in 14 years, and this would not be the year the streak ended, experts said. Much was made of Green Bay's defensive line, led by Reggie White and mammoth nose tackle Gilbert Brown. The Broncos' offensive line was seen as too small to compete with all that bulk and strength.

"Yeah, that fired us up quite a bit," Broncos offensive lineman Mark Schlereth said. "When you're reading every day how you're going to get pushed around and stomped on, you tend not to react very well to that. We knew, however, what we could do as a line. And we knew we had the best runner in the league behind us, and John Elway handing him the football. We knew we had a great team. But we also knew we had to prove it in the biggest game of the year. But I knew early on we were going to be able to move the football on them."

One of the more memorable aspects of the game was the nervousness exhibited by Elway's father, Jack. Sitting in the press box, Jack Elway was shown sometimes on the TV screen agonizing before big-play situations. Nobody wanted a championship more for John Elway than his dad.

Another unforgettable image was that of Gilbert Brown, gasping for air on the bench after several of the Broncos' sustained drives.

When Mobley made the clinching play, the weight of a thousand worlds was lifted off the Elways and everyone else who had lived and died with the Broncos. Morton was like anyone else rooting for the Broncos at that moment. When the clock hit all zeroes, he lifted his arms in the air and let out a yell.

"I had a lot of pride surge through me when we won it. As Elway put it so well, that win was for them, but also for all the other Bronco teams and the people of the Rocky Mountain region. I really thought that Bronco team was the best in football, and the reason I think they finally won it all was they had Terrell Davis. He was the guy that really put that team over the top. He was something to watch. But I was down on the field, and I'll never forget not long after the game when Elway and his wife, Janet, came by in a golf cart, being wheeled around to different places to do interviews. And somebody had already poured him a huge glass of a screwdriver, and it was just something to watch him be able to sit back and enjoy a win like that and relax with a drink and laugh. I thought, 'Boy, do I envy him' right now, because I would have been the same way had I won it. I remember asking John for a sip of that cocktail, and he gave it to me. It was a fun night for sure, and I just remember feeling very happy for John, to finally have gotten it after all those other Super Bowl losses. I could relate to him in that way, of course. So, I guess I got to live a little through him that night of what winning one was like. I would have preferred to have won one on my own, but that was still a great experience for me."

## The Helicopter Play

There is little question which play is most remembered from the Broncos' first Super Bowl victory.

On third down and 6 at the Green Bay 12-yard line, in a 17–17 game, John Elway was flushed from the pocket and took off for the goal line. The 1998 version of Elway was nowhere near as quick as the 1980s model, so it was a fairly lumbering No. 7 when he approached the crucial first-down mark, at the 6.

Elway dove for the first down, but right as he did two Packers defenders, LeRoy Butler and Mike Prior, hit him simultaneously.

Butler's hit to a mid-air Elway's shoulders sent him spinning clockwise, and he landed with a thud, right at the 6 with the ball still in his hands.

First down, Broncos. No chance, Packers. Not after Elway had survived the helicopter hit. He stood with a raised fist in the air, and let out a war cry to his teammates on the sidelines.

"That was the time where we knew we were going to win that football game," Broncos offensive lineman Mark Schlereth said. "I mean, there was just no way we were going to lose that game now and let him down."

What people forget is after Elway finished the drive with a touchdown to Terrell Davis, the Packers gave the ball right back to Denver, fumbling it away to Tim McKyer on the kickoff. Elway immediately went for the kill, throwing deep for another touchdown attempt.

Only trouble was, Green Bay's Eugene Robinson intercepted the pass, and Brett Favre took the Packers right down the field for the tying score. But that was the Packers' last good drive of the game. Elway atoned quickly for his shocking gaffe, leading Denver down for the winning drive, capped off by another Davis run. On Green Bay's final fourth-down play, Favre's pass over the middle was knocked down by John Mobley. Elway leapt to his feet safe in the instant knowledge that he was a world champion.

"Oh, baby, they're gonna win this thing!" Broncos play-by-play man Dave Logan yelled.

## Back-to-Back

The 1998 Denver Broncos were one of the great NFL teams of all time. There was definitely no championship hangover from the glorious season before. The Broncos played with a zeal that didn't let up until they sipped champagne again, after beating the Atlanta Falcons, coached by none other than Dan Reeves.

The Broncos won their first 13 games before dropping a 20–16 decision to the New York Giants. They lost the next week, too, to the Miami Dolphins, prompting worry among Bronco fans might have peaked too soon. They didn't.

They blasted the Dolphins in a playoff rematch, 38–3, and beat the New York Jets 23–10 to advance to the franchise's sixth Super Bowl. In a matchup that still seems too good to be true for its dramatic subplot, the Broncos played the Reeves-led Falcons in Miami.

How could this be scripted any better? John Elway vs. Dan Reeves, after all these years, in a game to decide a world championship.

The media tried mightily to get the feud between the two stirred up even more, but they were surprisingly low key in the week leading up to the game. The bigger controversy probably concerned Reeves' past relationship with Broncos coach Mike Shanahan.

Reeves told reporters he believed Shanahan had undermined his authority when he coached the Broncos, possibly conspiring with his good friend Elway to get him out. Reeves fired Shanahan in 1991 for presumably those reasons, but he was hired back as head coach in 1995.

Now, he, like Elway, had a chance at a measure of revenge against Reeves. In the end, both got it, with a 34–19 victory. Elway became, at 38, the oldest quarterback to win a Super Bowl MVP award, completing 18-of-29 passes for 336 yards, one touchdown pass, and one rushing score.

Elway had such an arsenal of offensive weaponry, it often seemed too easy for the Broncos. Davis had one of the greatest seasons in NFL history, rushing for a Bronco record 2,008 yards, on an astounding average of 5.1 yards per carry. He ran for 21 touchdowns and added two more on pass receptions, scoring 138 points.

Receivers Rod Smith and Ed McCaffrey each caught more than 1,000 yards worth of passes. The defense, led by veterans Bill Romanowski, Steve Atwater, and Trevor Pryce, was outstanding.

"Everything just went right for us all year long," kicker Jason Elam said. "We had a great team. Our offense was just unbelievable. They couldn't be stopped."

There was no gloating by Elway toward Reeves when Denver triumphed. Craig Morton remembers feeling good about that. He was friends with both men, but especially Reeves, and Morton knew he had to be hurting badly inside after a fourth Super Bowl defeat as a head coach.

"That was a game where I was definitely torn a little. Make that a lot. As a guy who loved being a Denver Bronco, naturally I was happy to see them win another Super Bowl. But Danny Reeves was and always will be my friend. It was tough to see him not get a championship again. You kind of wished both teams could have won, but of course that can't happen. The Broncos were just too good offensively in that game and that year. Davis was unstoppable and you could tell they were still hungry, to prove the one the year before wasn't a fluke. Elway had a great game and he was the perfect quarterback for that team. He could just stand in the pocket and throw to any number of quality receivers, or just give the ball to Davis and watch him run up the football field. Let me tell you, I was envious just watching him. Any quarterback would love to have a group of talent around him like he did."

After the win, the focus almost immediately shifted to one question: Would Elway come back for another season?

After several weeks of speculation, *The Denver Post's* Woody Paige one-upped the intense media competition for the answer to the question. After playing a round of golf in California with Elway, Paige wrote that the end was nigh for the Duke of Denver.

Elway confirmed Paige's scoop soon after, and at a Denver hotel conference room, on May 2, 1999, announced to the world he was retiring in an emotional address.

"I can't play football anymore," Elway said.

He might have wanted to keep playing, Elway said, but his body wouldn't let him anymore. After 16 years of thrills, the John Elway era was officially over.

## Elway: The Man

John Elway's name has been mentioned a lot in this book, but who was the real man behind the legend?

As we've seen, he was one of the most competitive men alive. He had great God-given talent. He is a Hall of Fame member and the greatest quarterback of all time, according to Craig Morton, who preceded him in Denver.

As perfect as Elway's life and career seemed, it was far from it. There were the blowout Super Bowl losses, of course, and a feud with his first NFL coach, Dan Reeves, that lasted for years. He lost his beloved father, Jack, not long after winning his first Super Bowl, then lost a twin sister to an early death soon after that. He divorced his first wife, Janet, and had to go through it all under a media glare that put some of the gory details in the public realm. He needed a knee replacement, and today walks with a pronounced limp.

Through it all, Elway has managed to crack his famous, toothy smile. Those teeth were often caricatured in the Denver papers, particularly by *Rocky Mountain News* cartoonist, Drew Litton.

*John Elway was always quick to crack his famous, toothy smile, which helped make him a favorite player in his college days at Stanford as well as in the media.* Photo courtesy of AP Images.

*Quarterback John Elway and coach Dan Reeves had distinctly different offensive philosophies. Elway wanted to throw the ball a lot more, and Reeves wanted to play a safe, conservative, running style.* Photo courtesy of AP Images.

Litton almost always portrayed Elway with big, protruding buck teeth, which annoyed the star quarterback greatly. He was called Mister Ed by some because of that, but never by reporters. Any such reference would have lead to an abrupt end of an interview.

Elway had moments of attitude and big-timed a few reporters along the way, but ask any of the people who played with him, and they say he never was anything other than one of the boys.

"A great teammate, great man," offensive lineman Mark Schlereth said.

"One of the greatest guys I've ever known and will know," kicker Rich Karlis said.

"Really, just a humble, down-to-earth guy," said another kicker, David Treadwell.

Evidence of Elway's lack of pretension goes back to his days at Stanford. Even though he was the hottest NFL prospect of his day, and a superstar on the Cardinal campus, Elway lived in a Spartan fraternity house room. He carried out weekly duties, such as cleaning toilets, just like any other brother.

On the football field, however, he was a star. He became one of the few college quarterbacks in history to earn All-America honors as a sophomore, setting numerous PAC-10 touchdown records—including six touchdown passes in a game against Oregon State. His junior year was less successful for the Cardinal team, including a 28–6 loss to San Jose State team coached by Elway's father. The senior season was better, but his final college game, against Cal, will always be remembered bitterly by Elway. On the last play of the game, a kickoff after Elway had just led the Cardinal to a scoring drive that put it up 20–19 with four seconds left, the Bears scored. This occurred after a miraculous series of laterals, followed by the Stanford band running onto the field and effectively acting as blockers against their own schoolmates. Cal's Kevin Moen ran past saxophonists, oboe and trombone players as he ambled into the end zone. It still ranks as probably the most unbelievable play of any kind in football history, pro or college.

The loss was devastating, as it kept Stanford out of a Bowl game, but Elway had lots to look forward to. Still, frat brothers called him Elwood and no amount of star treatment by the press gained him leverage over anybody else in the house. After he signed a $5 million contract with the Broncos, Elway returned to the house and was immediately given bathroom duty. His first night as a multi-millionaire was spent on the same waterbed he slept on as a poor college kid, with the same couple of posters on the wall serving as high-priced art in the room.

Elway met and fell in love with a pretty Stanford swimmer named Janet Buchan, and they married a year out of college.

Elway almost became a pro baseball player after leaving Stanford. During his sophomore season, the New York Yankees drafted him in the second round and gave him a $150,000 signing bonus. In the summer of 1982, Elway spent six weeks with the Yankees' Class-A team in Oneonta, New York, hitting .318 with 25 RBIs and no errors as an outfielder in 42 games.

By 1983, Elway was eligible for the NFL draft. The Baltimore Colts had the first pick, and made it clear to everyone they planned to take the blond quarterback out of Stanford. For the Colts, Elway would be the savior, the man to take them back to the championship days of Johnny Unitas. The local press predicted Elway would become as identified with Baltimore as crab cakes when his career was done.

But it never happened, all because of two men: Robert Irsay and Frank Kush. Irsay, the owner, was seen as an old-school, penny-pinching owner who treated players like cattle. Kush, the coach, was an abrasive, my-way-or-the-highway kind of guy who once slapped a player in a practice. Jack Elway reportedly despised Kush and advised his son in no uncertain terms never to play for him. Elway told the media he wouldn't sign with the Colts if they drafted him. He used his potential baseball career as discouragement to Baltimore management, but the Colts took him nonetheless. Elway was angry about it and made good on his promise to not even negotiate with the Colts. Baltimore had no choice but to entertain trade offers for Elway's rights. The Broncos quietly entered the bidding, with owner Edgar Kaiser leading the way. Prior to that, the Oakland Raiders nearly made the trade, but the deal fell apart when the third-party Chicago Bears asked for Raiders star defensive end Howie Long at the last moment.

Six days after the draft, on May 2, 1983, the Broncos persuaded Irsay to part with Elway for offensive tackle Chris Hinton, a 1984 first-round pick, quarterback Mark Herrmann, and $1 million cash.

Despite Hinton turning into a solid, multiple Pro Bowl player, the trade remains one of the greatest heists in sports history.

The trade created a sensation in Denver, instantly reviving the old orange madness-style hype of the first Super Bowl days. The Denver newspapers went into overdrive, and 53 media members attended Elway's first day of Broncos training camp, in the northern Colorado city of Greeley.

*The Denver Post* and *Rocky Mountain News* treated Elway's every utterance like it was from the Almighty Himself. The two newspapers were locked in a vicious, take-no-prisoners circulation war, and Elway single-handedly probably increased readership by at least 10 percent with his presence. Reporters were so afraid to get scooped on an Elway story that things reached absurd heights, such as the time the papers got into a sniping contest in print over what Elway had eaten for dinner at the chow hall one night. One paper reported Elway had green beans with his fried chicken; No, the other paper said, it was peas. This turned into an honest-to-goodness war of words between the two dailies at the time.

Some Bronco teammates became annoyed and even jealous at the attention Elway immediately received in that first training camp. Quarterback Steve DeBerg wasn't very hospitable to his rookie challenger. Other veterans, who'd felt shafted by management in money matters over the years, resented the huge contract given to a guy who had yet to play a down.

Elway, of course, wanted none of the media attention. Things got so bad, he begged the media to back off some, saying "I'm about to suffocate." But there was no chance of that. By saying he was suffocating, Elway created *another* angle for the press to attack. "Elway feels he's in a Denver fishbowl," became the angle for a fresh batch of stories.

In a 1989 *Sports Illustrated* story, Elway complained about it anew, saying: "They talk about my hair, they talk about my teeth, they talk about how much I tip, how much I drink…I'm sick of it."

Former *Rocky Mountain News* columnist Jay Mariotti, no stranger to bombast, took offense, then took it a step further by calling Elway a, "greedy and scared punk."

"Go ahead John, leave. Get out of Denver, baby. Go. You'll be crawling back here after a week."

On top of that, Elway had to deal with a coach, Reeves, who had distinctly different offensive philosophies. Elway wanted to throw the ball a lot more, and Reeves wanted to play a safe, conservative, running style. The two co-existed uneasily for years, until their unsavory parting.

But, fortunately, the two reconciled a couple years after Elway's retirement. In fact, Elway graciously invited Reeves to be part of his Hall of Fame induction entourage, and thanked him in his acceptance speech for the things he'd done for his career.

Through it all, Elway managed to keep his sanity. But it wasn't easy, especially having to deal with so much "star treatment" from the media and fans. In 1993, at the team hotel in Appleton, Wisconsin, prior to a game with the Packers, Elway was in an elevator with members of a wedding party. They asked the star quarterback if he could please, please join the reception. The bride and groom would be thrilled. Sorry, Elway said, he had a team commitment. Moments later, overcome by guilt, Elway showed up and posed for numerous pictures.

One of Elway's happiest times as a player, had nothing to do with the football field. Not long after one season, he took a trip to Germany, where he went unnoticed by anyone for several blissful days.

"John is a guy who just wants nothing more than to hang out with the fellas, have a couple of beers and have a lot of laughs," Karlis said. "He could be that way when it was just us, but he certainly couldn't be that way in any place that was too public. If he was out anywhere, he would get swarmed for autographs and people wanting to talk for a couple minutes and revel in his presence. That's just such a hard thing to live up to and have to deal with after a while. But John dealt with it about as well as you could ask of anybody. But I know it bothered him that so much focus was put on him, especially after victories where they'd say he won the game by himself or something. He knew football is a total team game, and he'd want other guys to get some pub, too. But when you're John Elway in Denver, that didn't happen much."

Said Schlereth: "When I think of John Elway, I don't think of the football player at first. I think of just the regular guy, the good friend who was just one of us and didn't want anything more than that. Then, I think of the football player—and that is quite a player."

Today, Elway keeps a much lower profile around Denver. He sold his interest in the several car dealerships that bore his name and doesn't make a big show about his ownership interest in the Colorado Crush of the Arena Football League. He also doesn't parade around town with flashy women on his arm, though he has remained Denver's most eligible bachelor since divorcing his first wife, Janet.

His name has been in the headlines recently mostly only through his son, Jack, who played quarterback for Denver's Cherry Creek High School. He was wearing the No. 7, of course. Elway served as an assistant coach for the team, and granted few interviews. Otherwise, Elway spends time with only a small circle of friends, although he has not given up making a dollar off his name entirely. He opened the John Elway Steakhouse in the Cherry Creek shopping district, not far from the one formerly owned by Denver's other No. 7 quarterback.

"And, surprise, surprise, his has been a big hit and mine was a flop," predecessor Craig Morton says. "Go figure. But let's face it, John Elway could put his name on a pile of cow dung and it would sell like crazy in Denver. But he's earned every penny he makes off his name. To have gone through life in that kind of a fishbowl in Denver, where he had absolutely no privacy if he went out at all is something I know I wouldn't have been able to handle. So, I guess I'm saying, 'Thank God I wasn't as good a quarterback as him.' He's the biggest star that Denver has probably ever had in any walk of life. But in the time I've known him and gotten to talk to him on occasion, he's remarkably down to earth. For a man who I've said is the greatest quarterback that ever played the game, he never let any of that go to his head or let it affect him as a person. And that's not easy to do, not when you do the things he accomplished."

## More Comebacks Than a Smart-mouthed Kid

Craig Morton had some great comebacks in his day. How about leading the Broncos to a 37–34 victory over Seattle in 1979, after the Broncos trailed 34–10 in the third quarter?

But Morton's didn't approach the number of his No. 7 successor, Elway. The Duke of Denver led an amazing 47 game-tying and game-winning fourth-quarter or overtime drives from 1983 to 1998. Denver's record in those games: 46–0–1.

"To me, that's just another reason why I pick Elway as the best quarterback ever," Morton said. "It wasn't just the things he could do as an athlete, things like throwing across his body for 60 yards. It was also his leadership and ability in the clutch. You could see the looks in the eyes of other teams when John had the ball in the last two minutes and the game was on the line. They expected something bad to happen to them, and it often did."

His first great comeback came against the team that drafted him, the Baltimore Colts, on December 11, 1983. Elway threw three fourth-quarter touchdown passes in a 21–19 win.

His last comeback was on September 15, 1996 against Tampa Bay, a 14-play, 80-yard fourth-quarter drive that gave Denver a 27–23 win.

Part of Elway's secret to success was that he never got bogged down with playbook minutiae. He improvised so well on any kind of busted assignment or coverage. He had such confidence that he could pull out any game that he didn't weigh himself down with lots of meek deference to the playbook. Many of his great fourth-quarter plays happened because Elway never got down or tentative as a player. He just got over the center for the next play and let 'er rip. No matter how badly things had gone to that point in a game, Elway's eyes always seemed to light up when he had the ball in his hands, with the game on the line, for a final possession.

"He had such an arm and so much quickness, he knew any one play might shut him down, but that it would be basically impossible to keep him down for a whole game," Morton said. "He just would say, 'Let's go back out there and just get open and I'll get the ball to you, no matter where you are.' He had that confidence in himself that you don't see in most guys. Not an overconfidence thing, as much as a belief that no matter what, they're not going to be able to stop you every time. I think the thing that I'll always remember about watching Elway play, in person from the sideline, was just how scared he made the other team, at all times. See, when you're as good as him, teams never let up, because they know they're going to get burned. He scared opposing coaches to death with how much he could do. I know if I had ever had to coach against him, my game plan would have just been prayer."

## 1990s And Beyond

After Elway retired in 1998, a young quarterback out of Michigan and son of an NFL Hall of Fame member was named his heir apparent.

Brian Griese was his name, and, while he had a couple of very good seasons with the Broncos, his time in Denver is generally regarded with disappointment.

Griese still holds the Bronco record for most games in succession with a touchdown pass (23), and the single-season high for completion percentage (66.7). But Griese never won a playoff game with the Broncos, and Denver's record in his first season as Elway's successor was 6–10.

Griese, whose father Bob won two Super Bowls with the Miami Dolphins, had two legends to try and live up to, and he always seemed burdened by the expectations. He was sometimes snippy with the media, once telling a reporter trying to joke about him being on his fantasy team: "I don't give a damn about your f*cking fantasy team."

Griese didn't help his cause, either, with some curious off-field incidents, including one night in 2002 when he fell in the driveway of teammate Terrell Davis during a party and was knocked unconscious. Griese said alcohol played no part, but the year before he was placed on probation after pleading no-contest to a charge of driving while impaired.

Griese's successor was the shaggy-haired, free-spirited Jake Plummer, a free-agent signee from Arizona. Plummer remains one of three Broncos quarterbacks to take the team to the AFC Championship, on January 22, 2006, after he bested New England's two-time defending Super Bowl quarterback, Tom Brady the game before.

But Plummer's career in Denver flamed out. He played poorly in the AFC title game loss at home to Pittsburgh, throwing two costly interceptions, and was largely ineffective in the '06 regular season. He lost his starting job late in the season to a rookie, Jay Cutler, and was out of the league by the next year.

Morton watched some of the games the two played, and feels a measure of sympathy for them.

"All I can say is I'm glad I didn't come to the Broncos after John Elway had played. That's a hell of a lot of pressure and expectation to have to live up to. The fact is, nobody could measure up to a John Elway. I know I couldn't have. Both those guys were good

*John Elways wasn't an easy act to follow. Quarterback Brian Griese never won a playoff game with the Broncos, and Denver's record in his first season as Elway's successor was 6–10.*

quarterbacks. I always liked the way Jake Plummer, especially, competed. And Brian Griese was a talented guy who did some good things. But if you didn't go to the Super Bowl in Denver, in those years after Elway, you were a failure. That's not fair, but nobody said life in the NFL is fair."

## How big did the Broncos become? Consider...

The Broncos sold 2,675 season tickets in their first season, 1960. By 2007, the number was 73,972. For the 2008 season, there were 23,000 names on a waiting list to buy season tickets.

The team was on pg. 3 of *The Denver Post* two days before that first game, the only story about the team in the paper. After they won the 1998 Super Bowl, *The Post* put out a 48–page section just on that one game.

Probably the most astonishing numbers are from television; Bronco games routinely get shares in the 70–80 percent range on the Denver network affiliate station. The competition is cutthroat to be known as the official Broncos station, which gains most regular-season broadcasts and exclusive locker-room post-game coverage.

In 1987, the last hour of the Denver-Cleveland AFC Championship Game achieved a 90-share of the Denver television market. That is believed to still be the largest local rating for any sporting event to ever be recorded by ACNielsen.

As we've seen, examples of Bronco-mania are already legend, but here are a few other stories of just how crazy, in the literal sense, Bronco fans have been: After a 33–14 loss to Chicago in 1973, in which the Broncos fumbled five times, a fan committed suicide and wrote, "I've been a Broncos fan since they were first organized, and I can't stand the fumbling anymore."

In 1977, a man named Rick Savage and his girlfriend dropped into a Denver bar for some drinks and dancing. Savage put money into a jukebox and moved to the music with his lady. Trouble was, the Broncos were on the TV at the bar, and the music overrode the sound. "Turn it down," one fan told Savage, who ignored him. The fan got up, unplugged the jukebox, then fatally shot Savage. "Nobody's going to mess with me when I'm watching the Broncos," the man reportedly said on his way to the slammer.

For the Denver media, the Broncos continue to be lifesaver. In an age of declining advertising revenues and media consolidation, the Broncos still deliver big numbers to Denver's newspapers and TV stations.

On a February day in 2008, two of the Top 10 most viewed stories on *The Post*'s website were related to the Broncos, nearly two months after their season had ended. When the season is in session, often the top two or three most clicked are Broncos stories.

Morton said he gets more requests to sign Broncos paraphernalia, by far, than the other two teams he played for.

"Bronco fans are literally everywhere. I don't care where it is I am, there's always a Bronco fan who I'll talk to. The team just has a very unique, passionate following. I know a lot of other teams have great fans, teams like Green Bay and Dallas and Washington, really passionate, great fans. But the passion of Bronco fans stacks up against anybody."

# chapter 7
# Stories, Opinions, and Other Thoughts

*"I always looked at him when he was first starting out and said, 'He's just going to be one of those guys that I'll always have to deal with in some way.'"*
—Craig Morton about Roger Staubach

## Practical Jokes Aplenty

One sign of a good team is how many practical jokers there are, and the number of their hijinks.

A team without some fun and laughs at each other's expense is likely to be a loser. Too many uptight players in the locker room, or one where the players don't feel close enough to play a joke on one another once in a while, can make for a dull, unexceptional team.

That was not the case with the Broncos in Morton's years in Denver. While not the bunch of pranksters like some of his former Dallas Cowboys teams, Morton's Broncos were teams that liked to have fun on and off the field.

Who was the biggest practical joker of them all?

"I would have to say Randy Gradishar. He was always very sly about it. He used to do a lot of things in training camp, like putting snakes in beds and other very unattractive looking bugs. You used to hear a lot of screams in the night. I was never the brunt of his deals, probably because I was the old man on the team. But I made sure that when my door was closed, it was locked. Because, I promise you, I was always looking over my shoulder. Jim Jensen was his cohort. They would plan all kinds of things.

"I was never much of a guy to play practical jokes on guys, but there was one guy I liked to 'goose' all the time, and that was our trainer, Steve Antonopulos. He was the goosiest guy in the world. That became my whole purpose in life for a while, figuring out new ways to goose him. Because, he was just so sensitive to any kind of goose. He would always let out some kind of squeal from the slightest touch. I would have elaborate ways to get him, like coat hangers on coat hangers, just stretched around corners, just to get him. I'd be on hands and knees, crawling on my belly, looking around corners when he was taping guys. He'd be looking for me every day, just to see what I would come up with next. I promise you, I got him every day. He would just make all kinds of noise.

*Randy Gradishar wasn't just an impressive linebacker, but also known as the team jokester. He was also named NFL Defensive Player of the Year in 1978 and is in the Broncos Ring of Fame.*

"But you can tell a close team by the number of practical jokes. When I played with the Giants, there weren't many, because I don't think many people liked each other. If you're on a successful team, guys are in a better mood and want to laugh more and have fun.

"One time, when I was a teammate with Steve DeBerg with the Broncos, we had a party where we all wore costumes, and you couldn't tell who was in them. I came as Father Time or something, and I forget what Steve came as, but when we went into the bathroom, we traded outfits. When we went back out, our wives didn't know who was who. And, we had a lot of fun playing with each other's wives! They had no idea we were a different person. Then, we finally had a time where we showed who we were, and they were quite shocked, to put it mildly.

"Another time, I had to go out and get Craig Penrose, who'd been drinking a little. That night, I ended up putting some fingernail polish on his finger and toenails. I waited until he fell asleep and painted him with red polish. When he got up in the morning, he didn't know shit, he was so hung over. But when he reached down to tie his shoes, he noticed they were bright red. That stuff is hard to get off, and he didn't have any turpentine or whatever to get it off. So, he had to go to practice with it still on."

After Gradishar retired in 1983, wide receiver Steve Watson became one of the practical-joke ringleaders. One day, Watson filled a bowl in the Broncos' locker room with what appeared to be Milk Duds. The outside of the snack items was chocolate-covered all right. But the inside was not chewy caramel. It was elk droppings.

"The really funny thing is, some guys chewed them and didn't seem to notice the difference," kicker Rich Karlis said.

## Some Cold Ones

Morton played in his share of cold-weather games in Denver, some in driving snow and temperatures that made the football feel like a rock.

But nothing ever topped the famous NFL Championship Game between the Dallas Cowboys and Green Bay Packers at Lambeau Field. The official temperature was minus-13, but the wind chill dropped it into the minus-40s.

"We went out to practice the day before and it was about 25 degrees. It wasn't anything bad at all. The next morning, we get a phone call in the room, a wake-up call, at the Holiday Inn in Oshkosh, Wisconsin. I roomed with Peter Gent, who wrote *North Dallas Forty*. The lady making the call says, "Good Morning Mr. Morton, Welcome to Oshkosh, Wisconsin. The temperature this morning is minus-18 degrees." And I said, 'Yeah, right. I'm not going to fall for this stuff.' I told Pete and we started laughing about it. We got dressed and went outside and absolutely just froze our asses off. We just thought this had to be a joke. It was really something unbelievable. Back in those days, I mean, we didn't have any cold weather gear. They had some tents on the sidelines that were about 70 degrees inside, but if you ever went inside there, you couldn't adapt coming out.

"Warming up on the field before the game, I just wondered how the hell I was going to throw this rock. That's the only time in my whole athletic career where I said, 'Please god, don't let [Don] Meredith get hurt.' If you look at the films of that game now, they noticed that when Bob Hayes, when he wasn't going to be in a play, he would tuck his hands inside his pants. The Packers noticed that, and so they knew they could go into a different defense when he did that. That hurt us some, but there was just no way to keep warm in that game. We only had some flimsy Dallas Cowboys jackets, but they wouldn't keep you warm. Guys ended up wrapping tape all over their heads, to try and get some warmth there. You could see them with little slits around the eyes. We looked like mummies."

## No Stickum

In Morton's day, lots of players pasted themselves with a trademarked brand of glue called Stickum. Receivers mostly used it, but some, such as Oakland defensive back Lester Hayes, took it to the extreme.

Morton detested Stickum, and would go to the referee anytime it got on the football and have it replaced before he took another snap.

"You couldn't believe the places where some guys had Stickum. I hated it. Every time we played against Oakland especially, I would always tell my center, 'You feel any of that stuff on the ball, you tell me and we'll replace it.' If you took a snap and got that stuff on your hands, you couldn't rotate the ball in your hand fast enough to get it to a spot where you could throw it."

Stickum was eventually outlawed by the NFL.

## Don't Bank With The Owners

Morton laughs, or wants to cry, when he thinks back to some of his naïve behavior when he first came into the NFL. Especially when it came to money, and how he thought he and some Dallas Cowboys teammates could outsmart general manager Tex Schramm.

"Lee Roy Jordan, Bob Lilly, and I held out for more money. But Schramm, when he signed us all, he made sure we opened accounts in the bank that he had interest in, Park Cities Bank. So, the Cowboys knew exactly every penny we had, how long we could hold out. We were such dumbshits. I lasted the longest, but they just picked us off. They just knew, 'Well, he's got to pay his mortgage on such and such a date, so we'll just wait.' That happened to a lot of Cowboys players in the early years, because they all did their banking at Park Cities Bank. We were never smart enough to know that."

## Wives Know All

Talk to most married pro athletes, and they'll give a knowing nod when the subject of wives comes up. Namely, there isn't a single thing they don't know about every player on the team, all their foibles, virtues, and anything else.

"They knew everything. My ex-wife, Susan, would come home and tell me some things and I'd be like, 'How in the world did you know this stuff?' They didn't have another life. All they had was to talk about everybody else and what they were doing. It was the gossip train. But the truth is, I didn't blame them. Football is a very self-indulgent sport for the players. The wives, they don't get to really share a lot of things, except the gossip. Some of the stories would just grow and grow into an immense tale. What sagas they could get to.

"But we really didn't have a lot of catty wives in Denver. But when I was with the Cowboys, guys would always use me as an excuse, because I was single. I would get phone calls around the clock from wives, wondering where their husbands were. I would always be, 'Well, he just left.' And, I had no idea. I would always go in the next morning and say, 'Okay, if you're going to use me as a beard, shit, tell me this. I don't know what to say to your wife.' All the guys would say, 'Well, I'm going over to Craig's.' I was used. So, the wives would love me for being the nice single guy, but also hate me because all the guys were supposedly coming over to my place all the time."

"Marriage is tough, but it's even tougher being married to a pro athlete. There is always some way the guy can escape from reality, either to a game or a practice or a meeting or an endorsement thing or whatever. They never really have to face what's really going on at home, and the reality of what it's like to actually be married. Athletes get a free ride for so long and then a light goes off in their head where it's like, 'Oh, there really is a commitment to this marriage thing.' Athletes never want to face reality if it's unpleasant."

## Tough Runners

The Broncos of Morton's years never had a dominant running back. But what they lacked in superstar talent, they made up for in pure toughness.

"I mean, they were really tough guys. Jon Keyworth, Lonnie Perrin, Rob Lytle, Rick Parros, Larry Canada, they all just really worked their asses off. They just came rumbling up to the line and would just beat the dirt to get another yard or two. They were a big reason why we won so many games. They didn't fumble a lot and always got the tough yards. They made me want to work my ass off for them. That's what makes a good team, guys working for each other."

## No Kidding On This One

When John Elway came to the Broncos, he had recently lost the last college game he ever played for Stanford. It was to Morton's alma mater, Cal, in a 1982 game that will forever be known for its last-second, multi-lateral Cal touchdown. That, and the fact that the Stanford band came onto the field during the play, thinking the game was won for the Cardinal.

Morton coached the Broncos quarterbacks briefly in Elway's second season. Did he ever kid him about the band game?

"Well, I might have mentioned it to him. But I didn't get into too much detail with him. I still wanted to be able to talk to him, so I didn't pursue it much!"

## The Quarterbacks Of Today: Too Protected?

It might sound odd coming from a man who took many huge hits in his career, plenty of them that would be considered cheap or dirty in today's NFL: but Morton would not want to play under today's rules, which are designed to better protect the quarterback.

"I don't like that there are basically different rules for a quarterback. I liked it when it was the same for everybody. Jack Lambert said about 10 years after he retired, after watching a game, that it seemed like the quarterbacks had dresses on, because you couldn't touch them. I think I agree with a lot of that. Not to disparage today's quarterbacks' toughness. But it's just that they get some different rules applied to them, and I'd rather see everybody have the same standards when it comes to hitting and the tougher aspects of football. If I played today, I wouldn't want any favoritism."

## Parents Were Part Of The Package

In the three NFL cities in which Morton played, he always made sure to bring his parents along. He helped pay off the family house in Campbell with his first big contract, and took care of the rental payments in Dallas, New York, and Denver.

"Even after my career ended, when I moved up to Portland for a while, I moved 'em up there. So they were always around me. One of my deals was to always take care of them.

My parents were always known by their middle names, and they named me Larry Craig. So, I became Craig Morton. But my dad's real name was Charles Kenneth and mom was Kerry Maxine. But, if I ever want to be anonymous, I can just go as Larry Morton. It's on my driver's license, and it's really come in handy a few times."

Morton's parents are now deceased, as well as a sister. His mother and one of his three sisters died within a few months of each other nearly six years ago, from pancreatic cancer—a time Morton calls it one of the toughest in his life.

## Pro Sports And Marriage: Not Easy

Marriage is not easy. For anybody. Half of all marriages end in divorce and, the joke goes, the other half wish they could, but don't have the energy to start over.

It's no secret, certainly among pro athletes, that the divorce rate is a little higher. You're a young man, making lots of money, in the spotlight, in the best shape of your life—things can happen.

Morton was married from 1977 to 1993 to Susan Sirmen, then they divorced. He remarried in 2007 to a woman, Kym, he'd been dating for seven years, and thinks he finally got it right. "She is the light of my life," beams Morton.

Morton is not afraid to publicly admit he was not immune to the temptations of stardom, of being an NFL quarterback.

"I admit to all my flaws now as a person. I've always been a very closed person, where people didn't know a lot of things about me. I was never a person to brag about anything, or make myself above anybody.

"But I can say now—and I don't want to embarrass my ex-wife—but, I was a very good father, and not a very good husband. It still is haunting to me a lot of times, that I was such an ass. Sometimes, in the mornings now, I'll think, 'Geez, how could I do some of the stuff I did?' But then I'll just keep talking to myself and say, 'Well, you did it, and maybe you can help someone else going through the same thing or whatever. Just try to be better going forward.' A lot of it is just male ego. You have a lot of things thrown at you or given to you, and it's a temptation thing. The guys that are able to stay faithful, you admire the hell out of them after it's all done. I guess it's a thing where you just think you want to have all the fun you can. But it's a weakness, and I wish I could do a lot of it over again.

"I was not a guy who could even think of going out on the road and having a few drinks on the night before a game. I always just knew I had a game the next day, and I couldn't understand the guys who could do that. So, that wasn't my downfall about being on the road. I just couldn't fathom trying to have to play while being hung over, but I saw a lot of guys do that. But if you want to say I had my fun, or what I thought was fun, on the road then, I did. But I look back on it now, and it was asinine."

Morton had two children with Susan—a son, Michael, and a daughter, McKenna. Morton makes clear that it was never Susan's fault for any of his actions, and adds that he wouldn't be half the person he is today without her.

"Of all the great people that have come into my life, Susie was the most important. She was the first person who challenged my beliefs and directions. If it wasn't for her, 1977 would not have been possible."

Morton continues, "The great moments that we had and the lives of our children are not a theme of this book, but in my heart we enjoyed the best moments ever. She is a light and gift from God, and has given me so much, not the least of which being two parts of my heart—Michael and McKenna."

## Sunday Afternoon Victory=Football Heaven

Ask any football player, and they'll tell you some of the happiest memories of their lives were on the Sunday nights after a victory.

Most teams gather together at a local establishment after a victory, to eat and drink and relive the glories of a few hours earlier. The Broncos of Morton's era were no exception. But they were notable in that they would still usually hang out as a team after a loss—although there weren't many of them in Morton's time.

After home games—and often after road ones, as the Broncos chartered to Denver right after road contests—the team gathered at Colorado Mine Company, a restaurant in Glendale run by Buck and Cindy Scott that was favored by visiting celebrities such as Elvis Presley.

"They would have a room set up in the back for us, and the whole team and their families would hang out. It was wonderful. And they would also have a TV set up that would replay the game. Don't forget, this was back in the days when VCRs and things like that weren't very common. So, to see the game so quickly after you'd just played was pretty revolutionary. Of course, after a win, it was much more fun in there. And we had a lot of them."

## I'm Talking To Somebody Here!

When Morton was first hired by the Denver Gold of the United States Football League, to succeed Red Miller as coach, he was at a party of sorts to celebrate and was approached by longtime Denver sportscaster Mike Nolan for a comment.

Nolan, live on the air, sidled up to Morton and asked for his thoughts on his new job. Morton, in a conversation with someone and unaware of who was tapping him on the shoulder, turned around and yelled 'I'm talking to somebody here!'

After an awkward few moments, Morton sheepishly realized the situation and gave the interview.

## Dorsett Does Denver

On June 3, 1988, the Broncos acquired running back Tony Dorsett from the Dallas Cowboys, for a future draft choice. The deal made big news in Denver and around the NFL. *Sports Illustrated* put Dorsett on its cover, with the headline "Happy To Be A Bronco, Buster." *The Sporting News* made him a cover boy too, with a "Dorsett Does Denver" header.

*As a Dallas Cowboy rookie, running back Tony Dorsett scored a touchdown against the Broncos in Super Bowl XII. In 1988, he became a Bronco himself and led the team in rushing, with 703 yards and five touchdowns.*

Dorsett, the Broncos hoped, would be the kind of back that could put them over the hump for a Super Bowl title—after two blowout losses in recent years. It didn't exactly turn out that way. The Broncos went 8-8, their first non-winning season in six years. But Dorsett was not a total bust with the Broncos. He actually led the team in rushing, with 703 yards and five touchdowns. He also had two 100-plus yard rushing games and caught 16 passes.

However, Elway had one of the worst years of his career, throwing 19 interceptions to 17 touchdowns, and the defense wasn't good at all. The team allowed 40 points or more three times, including an embarrassing 55–23 loss at Indianapolis in week 9. Dorsett came into training camp, after 11 years in Dallas, in great spirits. The man who scored a touchdown against the Broncos in Super Bowl XII as a rookie still ran a 4.38 40-yard dash. He had lost his starting job to Herschel Walker with the Cowboys, after running for 12,036 yards in those 11 years. He had also been through a number of personal and professional problems, including his name being mentioned in a federal drug investigation. He had problems with the IRS, which placed liens on two of his homes, and he lost $600,000 on an oil investment in 1984. But Dorsett did make one good last financial decision, which was to accept a $6 million annuity from the Cowboys in 1985, in lieu of receiving an instant raise. Beginning in 1995, Dorsett began receiving the first of 20 annual checks worth $180,000. Entering 2008, Touchdown Tony still had eight years' worth of checks coming from the Cowboys.

Dorsett chose Denver as a new team largely because of Dan Reeves, who was his offensive coach for a few years in Dallas. Morton was the quarterbacks coach that year, and thinks Dorsett performed well in his final NFL year. He was on injured reserve with the Broncos in 1989.

"Tony was playing pretty well for us, but then he hurt a knee late in the year and that was pretty much it for him. He came to the Broncos pretty much because of Froggy (Reeves). I enjoyed getting to know him a little bit that one year we were together.

"Obviously, we talked a little bit about Super Bowl XII, but he enjoyed talking about it a little more than I did!"

## Sell It!

How competitive was John Elway?

"Oh my God, very competitive," Morton said. "Most pro athletes are, but John was in just such a foul mood anytime he lost at anything. When I first met him, I could tell this was a guy who would be like that."

Later in his career, Elway stocked his game room at his Cherry Hills, Colorado, home with a pool table, and reigned as undefeated champion. That is, until backup quarterback Bubby Brister showed up one night.

Brister was the first to beat Elway on his own pool table. It happened on a Saturday night. By Monday morning, the pool table was gone. Elway sold it, disgusted by its sight after the loss.

## Rocky Mountain Altitude—Myth Or Factor?

Ask any athlete in Denver, and they'll probably tell you: the mile-high altitude that generates so many out-of-town headlines isn't that big a deal.

Experts say any pro athlete is usually in good enough condition, so that it isn't a factor. But the Broncos always encouraged the writers to make a big deal out of it, Morton said.

"We would always say, 'Keep writing about that altitude!' It would play on the minds of opponents. They would always talk about it, and how you had to really prepare for it, and it worked to our advantage the more they did that. You would see teams bring oxygen masks, and guys sucking on them after a play. I mean, I never once used an oxygen mask in Denver. I think teams would out-think themselves over the altitude. If you were totally out of shape, you might notice it, for sure. But otherwise, it was all a mental thing. I still get a kick when I see stories of teams talking about the altitude and how they have to really deal with it."

## First Touchdown Pass in The Swamp

Craig Morton could be the answer to a lot of trivia questions, but one real good one is: he threw the first touchdown pass for the Giants in Giants Stadium history. In 1976, Morton threw the pass to Giants receiver Jimmy Robinson, in their home opener against his previous team, Dallas.

"That was the good news," said Morton. "The bad news is, we still got our butts kicked."

In fact, the Giants would lose their first nine games of the '76 season. Head coach Bill Arnsparger was fired after seven games, replaced by John McVay.

That Giants team had the 33-year-old Morton as the starting quarterback, but he could have been called "Kid" next to backup Norm Snead, who was 37.

"We were the Geritol® backfield," Morton quipped. "We also had Larry Csonka on that team, and Larry was no spring chicken by that point. But I'll tell you what, Larry could still punish would-be tacklers. He'd lower his shoulder and still just be able to carry guys along with him. But our offensive line didn't give him much daylight to run."

Speaking of trivia involving that '76 team: the Giants had a linebacker, Brad Van Pelt, whose son, Bradlee, would play briefly for the Broncos. Bradlee Van Pelt is the answer to a good trivia question, which is: Who was the quarterback to complete the last pass to Hall of Fame member Jerry Rice?

On September 2, 2005, Van Pelt completed a pass to Rice in a preseason game. Three days later, Rice retired.

## No Guilt

Ask Morton if he ever felt guilty about the attention he got as a quarterback, and the answer is a quick, "Hell no!"

"Yeah, the quarterback probably gets more attention and praise than he deserves when things are going good. But he also gets more of the blame than he deserves when things are going bad. It works both ways. When Woody Paige starts getting on you, hell, you deserved those good accolades! You're either in the penthouse, or the outhouse. But, I would always feel a little uncomfortable if I got too much press after a win or a good stretch of games. Football is such a team sport, that you're only as good as the guy next to you. If one guy doesn't block, or another doesn't run his route correctly, or whatever it is, you can't have much individual success and you sure as hell don't have much team success. All you have to do it look at Tom Brady in the most recent Super Bowl (New England's loss to the Giants in 2008). The offensive line couldn't protect him in that game, and he couldn't do anything. It takes 11 guys all pulling together for any one guy to shine."

## Don't Bet On It

After he was hired by his college alma mater to work as a major gifts officer—"which means I ask for money for a living," Morton says with a chuckle—his name briefly surfaced in what seemed at first blush to be a gambling scandal. Morton, for a time in the 1990s, was the celebrity picker of pro football games for a gambling service. It was a harmless endeavor, with Morton having almost no more knowledge of the games he was picking than if, say, Bill Gates was doing it.

But when Morton was named one of 114 voters in the Harris Interactive Poll, which largely determines the teams playing in the Bowl Championship Series, the NCAA came calling to ask of Morton's involvement with the gambling service. The NCAA quickly absolved Morton of anything, but Morton called it a "bizarre deal" that aggravated him at first.

"Sometimes, you just never know what's out there about you, especially with all this Internet age stuff."

## Fundamentals: Gotta Have 'Em

When Morton played at Cal, if he made a mistake, he would have to run the 100-yard dash 10 times after practice. What the coaching staff most watched out for were footwork mistakes, and Morton had the fundamentals drilled in him to the point where he literally would do them in his sleep.

"1–2–3 left, 1–2–3 right, half a step up in the pocket—things like that. You never forgot those footwork fundamentals. The thing that is hurting quarterbacks from getting to the pros now is that a lot of them come from the spread offense, and have never been under a center. When I saw Alex Smith come out of Utah, and was the No. 1 choice in the draft with the 49ers, I (found out) he'd never taken a snap from under center. Well, this is a whole new game in the NFL, where you have to be under the center and get the game from that focus. I knew he was going to have difficulties because of that. You've got to be able to see the reads, you've got to notice things on the line, all kinds of things."

## San Diego Chargers: How Did They Not Win It All?

Morton said that he is most surprised that the San Diego Chargers never made it to the Super Bowl in the early 1980s. After all, one would think a team with such stars as Dan Fouts, Charlie Joiner, Kellen Winslow, John Jefferson, and Chuck Muncie should have won a championship.

"I mean, Fouts was a great passer, and a tough SOB. They had some outstanding players on that team and I remember thinking that team would win a few rings. But somehow it didn't happen. I mean, they had a lot more talent than teams, but talent doesn't always do it. But honestly, that team had so many weapons. They could move the ball up the field just so fast, it would just make your head spin. Fouts was one of the great timing passes who ever lived. He had an unbelievable grasp of the game and Don Coryell was one of the great offensive minds in the game.

I guess their defense wasn't quite good enough when all was said and done but, boy, I really thought that team would win a couple of Super Bowls."

## The *Hee Haw* Girls

As we've already seen, Morton freely admitted to enjoying his bachelor years in the NFL. He had plenty of teammates who enjoyed them as well, but Roger Staubach wasn't one. Morton found that out one night around Los Angeles, when, during training camp, he and Cowboys teammate Walt Garrison went to meet a couple of women who appeared on the popular TV show *Hee Haw*.

"Walt knew these girls in Los Angeles and asked if I wanted to come out to some country club and we'd all have dinner together. I said, 'Hell, I'm in.' We ended up having this great dinner with a lot of wine, and it was wonderful."

The coaches ended up finding out about their trying to smuggle the ladies back to their dorm room, however, not only breaking that team rule but also busting curfew. Morton tried to hide the two women under some clothes, on a ledge in the room, but was busted by a coach doing bed checks. Morton ended up being fined $1,500 and said Garrison "still owes me $750" because he couldn't squeal on his teammate.

When the girls were back at the hotel, Morton stopped by quarterback Roger Staubach's room to introduce them.

"This one girl I introduced him to was a total knockout. Well, the first thing Roger instinctively does is get up and take a picture out of his wallet and say: 'Let me show you a picture of my wife and kids.' And that's what he did. Unbelievable. But that's the kind of guy he was, and I respected the hell out of him. He walked his walk, believe me. He's an amazing guy, and (has) been a great friend to me.

"Roger and I played against each other in college, and we beat them (Navy) when they were a highly ranked team. And we played against each other in a college all-star game, and by the time we were in Dallas and on the same team together, we still were competing against each other. I always looked at him when he was first starting out and said, 'He's just going to be one of those guys that I'll always have to deal with in some way.' It just seemed he was always there, going for the same things I was all the time. We went back and forth a lot in Dallas, where I'd be the starter, then he would. But through it all, Roger was and still is just a class guy and one of the great quarterbacks that ever played the game."

## Marriage, During The Season

When Morton got married on November 7, 1977, to Susan Sirmen, it raised many eyebrows, and not just because it seemed he would forever be the confirmed bachelor.

The Broncos were still playing football when the wedding happened. Originally, Morton told her he'd walk the aisle "after the Super Bowl," which started out as a joke. But with the Broncos looking certain to make the playoffs, and the possibility of a run to the Super Bowl very much there, the couple decided they didn't want to wait that long to get hitched.

"We got married in Dallas, and it was an unbelievable wedding. But I had to get up and get ready for practice the next day. Then we had the playoffs coming up, so the honeymoon was delayed a little!"

The honeymoon took place in Hawaii, a few days after Super Bowl XII.

## Always Time For An Autograph

Morton has never, ever, turned down an autograph request. That is saying something for a guy who was a pretty big star in his time, and played 18 years at football's highest level. Why hasn't he ever said no?

"Because, when I was a young kid, probably in the sixth or seventh grade, I used to go to Cal-Stanford games. I was a very shy kid, and one time at one of their games there were a bunch of kids going up for autographs and, man, I was lagging behind because I didn't have enough courage to ask anybody. I went up to this one guy and said, 'Can I have your autograph' and he said 'I don't have any time, kid.'

"It hurt my feelings so much that I went behind a tree and cried and cried. I said 'God, if you ever let me be somebody special like that, I promise I'll never decline an autograph request to anybody.' And, I never have."

## Marketing Heaven

There may never have been a better sales boost given to a product—in the history of soda pop, at least, than when the Broncos' defense was nicknamed the Orange Crush in 1977.

For the next two years, there was no question as to the best-selling soda brand in Denver. It was Orange Crush, a soda that had been around for decades, but received a priceless amount of free advertising when the Broncos ascended to power.

In 1906, a man named J.M. Thompson created the original patent for Orange Crush soft drink, in Chicago. In 1916, the company was incorporated in Los Angeles, and was advertised soon after as Ward's Orange Crush, after Neil Callen Ward, who perfected the beverage's formula.

The company had several owners after that, including Pepsi, Procter and Gamble, and Cadbury Schweppes. By the mid-'70s, it was a decent seller in the soft drink market, but things exploded along with the Broncos' good fortunes and the nickname.

The regular, corporate Orange Crush logo was incorporated onto Broncos T-shirts that sold into the tens of thousands by the time of the team's '77 playoff run. The Denver market was infiltrated with just as many over-orders of the actual soda, and it flew off store shelves.

"It was unbelievable, it was just everywhere. That's all anybody drank in Denver," Morton said. "I still have several bottles of it somewhere at home. I'll never drink it!"

Orange Crush dominated sales in Denver and much of the Rocky Mountain West, but began to fade as did the team's fortunes by the early '80s. Still, many Denverites still like to keep a six-pack around in their refrigerators, just to remember the good times.

"They put out some special Bronco editions," Morton said. "I imagine there are quite a few cases of that stuff in many people's basements still."

## Movie Star? Not Quite

Those who have seen the 1988 film, *Everybody's All-American* might have noticed a Denver Broncos player, wearing the No. 7. That is Craig Morton, but don't look for his name in the credits.

Director Taylor Hackford used stock footage of some Broncos games in the film, which centers around the life of the character, Gavin Grey, portrayed by Dennis Quaid. The Grey Ghost is a conflicted quarterback who finished up his career with the Broncos, after a spectacular college career. Quaid's character wears the No. 7 in the film, and some game-action footage of him in action is Morton, from real NFL games.

"They actually called me and asked if I minded if they used some footage of me. I said certainly not. There's actually another movie where I'm in, when I played with the Giants."

That film is the 2006 Mark Wahlberg vehicle, *Invincible*, about the life of a 1970s Philadelphia Eagles player named Vince Papale.

"I also did a commercial once with Ricardo Montalban. And I did a thing with Bill Bixby once on TV. But I can't even remember what it was for. Trust me, it was nothing too big, and nobody was too impressed with my acting abilities."

## The Jockey® Ad

In 1976, when he was with the Giants, Morton was talked into doing an advertisement for the Jockey underwear company. Much to his later dismay, Morton can be forever seen in a pair of skimpy white briefs in the ad, which also features athletes such as Lou Brock, Jim McMillian, Ed Marinaro, and Vic Hadfield.

"Oh my God. I remember when I left the shoot, thinking, 'Wait a minute, this could be really embarrassing.' They never told me at the time what the shot would look like. But when it came out, yeah, I took some ribbing from the boys. Jim Palmer was the guy who made all the money in those deals, and none of the rest of us did. But, hey, I can laugh about it now. Those were the times. Those were what guys wore back in those days. Hell, I wouldn't mind looking like that now."

## College Game Wins Out

Morton doesn't watch a lot of pro football today, except for perhaps some big playoff games. Part of the reason, he says, is because he likes watching the college game so much more.

"I just think the NFL has been so stubborn about not adopting some of the great rules that make football really good, and college football has the best rules. Things like stopping the clock when you make a first down in the last two minutes; the timeouts they automatically take if they want to review something, whereas in the pros you have to wait for some guy to grab some dumb red flag out of his sock. It's humiliating to see a coach have to do that. The overtime rule is so much better in college than the pros, too. It's so unfair that a team has the advantage just because it won a coin toss. That's just not fair. The college way, both teams get an equal chance to win in overtime. To me, it just makes for such a more enjoyable experience to watch."

## In Morton's Footsteps—Sort Of

What is interesting about the post-NFL careers of Craig Morton and John Elway is how they got involved with football in different leagues.

Morton coached the Denver Gold of the USFL. Elway became a part owner of the Colorado Crush of the Arena Football League. Elway originally was rumored to be a possible part-owner of an NFL team that would return to Los Angeles, but nothing materialized. He also briefly considered being part of a group to bid on the Denver Nuggets, Colorado Avalanche, and the Pepsi Center—a package eventually sold to Missouri real estate developer, Stan Kroenke, also the husband of one of the Walton sisters and heir to the massive Wal-Mart fortune.

Elway oversaw a Crush team that won a championship, and one look at him in the owner's box at games makes it clear he takes the outcome very seriously. Losing, even as a rich owner of failed NFL prospects, seems to hurt as bad as any of his NFL days. Well, maybe that's a slight exaggeration, but remember, this is a guy who sold a pool table of his after losing for the first time on it.

## If Only Morton Had A Sharp(i)e

Ask Morton one player he would loved to have had in his huddle and he names longtime Bronco tight end, Shannon Sharpe.

"What a great athlete he was—one of the best tight ends ever. He was a tight end who could block and catch the tough short passes, but had wide receiver speed."

Sharpe played 12 of his 14 NFL seasons with the Broncos, and retired as the league's all-time yardage leader for a tight end (10,060).

His play was sometimes overshadowed by his flamboyant commentary, including the time during a preseason game in Australia when he slammed the country for its lack of taxicabs, and for mocking the New England Patriots in a Broncos blowout victory by pretending to call the President to "send in the National Guard" to get the Pats some relief.

Sharpe, a regular on Denver's two Super Bowl-winning teams, signed as a free agent with the Baltimore Ravens in 2000, after the Broncos foolishly tried to low-ball him on a new contract. How did that work out for Denver? Not too well.

The Broncos played the Ravens in a playoff game that year, and lost, with Sharpe catching a long touchdown pass. Baltimore went on to win a Super Bowl, and the Broncos got him back in 2002 and he caught 123 more passes for Denver in two years before retiring. Today, he is a popular studio analyst with CBS.

## Morton's Teammates, Elway's Heroes

Two of the players Elway most idolized growing up were two of Morton's teammates with the Cowboys, Calvin Hill and Roger Staubach.

"Calvin Hill was one of the top running backs in the NFL in his prime. I handed off a lot of footballs to him, and I mean, he was a great talent," Morton said.

Elway admired Staubach for his scrambling ability. In Staubach's day, he was considered the NFL's best at wriggling out of trouble in the backfield, with the possible exception of Fran Tarkenton. Hence the nickname "Roger the Dodger."

Trivia time: Who was the roommate of Hill's wife, Janet, at Wellesley? Answer: Hillary Rodham.

## Other Memorable Broncos, On And Off The Field

No book about the Broncos would be complete without mentioning a few of the memorable players who came after Morton's time in Denver.

Probably chief among them is a linebacker out of Boston College named Bill Romanowski.

Romanowski was an excellent player, arguably of Hall of Fame caliber. He started on Denver's two Super Bowl-winning teams and won another ring with San Francisco. But, unfortunately for him (or maybe not), he probably is best remembered today for using an astonishing array of supplements. Some were natural, many were not. In a first-person biography, Romanowski admitted to using steroids and human growth hormone—which may or may not have helped explain his often wild, manic nature on the field. Romanowski talked trash with anybody, and even spit on a player, J.J. Stokes of the 49ers, in a memorable 1997 *Monday Night Football* game.

Romanowski's sterling career ended in tatters. He was suspended by the NFL in 2003 while with Oakland, after steroids were found in a drug test. He punched a Raiders teammate, Marcus Williams, and was ordered to pay $340,000 for his lost wages and medical bills.

But whatever one wants to call Romanowski, a loser as a player can't be one of them. He was a punishing hitter, and even though he dished out plenty physically and verbally, he never whined when people gave it back to him as hard. In fact, he liked opponents who pushed him to the limit, who best tested his fine abilities.

"He played the game hard, bottom line," Broncos teammate Mark Schlereth said. "You didn't like Romo at all as an opponent, and sometimes not even as a teammate. But you respected his abilities, and he helped us win two Super Bowls."

Speaking of characters, Schlereth qualifies.

As of 2008, the former Bronco offensive lineman had undergone 29 surgeries. Most were to his knees, but several were to his back. In almost every one of Schlereth's off-seasons in the NFL, he had at least one surgery.

"It was just part of the summer routine," he said.

A native of Anchorage, Alaska, Schlereth was a quotable, friendly player who played on an offensive line that severely discouraged members from talking to the press. Those who did were fined and/or reprimanded in a kangaroo court, but Schlereth couldn't help it a few times.

No wonder he went on to a lucrative, post-playing career as an ESPN analyst and a soap opera star. In 2007, he landed a regular role as Detective Roc Hoover on the popular *Guiding Light.* Somehow, he transformed himself from grunty-looking offensive lineman to sculpted, waxy-looking leading man. But all his teammates will always refer to him by his football nickname "Stink." Not because of a foul body odor, although he didn't smell like fresh daisy after games, but because of a restaurant job his sister had where some of her duties included cutting the heads off slimy, smelly fish and serving them as delicacies called "stinkheads." When teammates found out, they tagged him with the name and it stuck.

Schlereth finally couldn't do it anymore by 2001, and retired a Bronco. Coach Mike Shanahan saluted him for his toughness, saying he had probably the highest pain threshold of any player he ever coached.

Another interesting character who wore the orange and blue is kicker Jason Elam. Not only was he a multiple Pro Bowl player and co-owner of the NFL record for longest field goal in league history (63 yards, with Tom Dempsey), Elam is a pilot and author. His 2007 novel *Monday Night Jihad* was a local best-seller, a book that combined football with terrorism and…spirituality. Some of Elam's more interesting life experiences include the time in Alaska when the plane he piloted was forced into an emergency landing in a field, a field that included one angry bear. Elam might have been luckier to escape the bear than a serious accident from the landing.

Elam tied Dempsey's 28-year-old record on October 25, 1998, with four seconds left in the first half of a game at home with Jacksonville. The Broncos had just been hit with a five-yard penalty, making what had originally been a long field goal attempt seem unthinkable. But when Elam answered "I think so" to coach Mike Shanahan's question if he had enough leg to make it, out he went. Despite a high snap, Elam got all of the football and it slipped barely over the crossbar. Today, the ball and Elam's right shoe sit in the Hall of Fame in Canton.

Wide receiver Rod Smith, a probable Hall of Fame player some day, was a unique individual. Undrafted out of college, Smith always carried a simmering resentment of spoiled first-rounders, which he used to his advantage. After establishing himself as a star, Smith loosed the occasional verbal barb at teammates or opponents who he felt didn't match his work ethic or who got undeserved attention.

One year, a reporter asked Smith what he thought of the Broncos' newest draft picks.

"Dude, I don't watch," Smith said. "I'm still kind of bitter. Some guys got drafted and they ain't played football in 15 years and I'm still waiting to get drafted. I'm still waiting to hear my name."

Smith posted 70 or more catches from 1997 to 2005, and is the Broncos' all-time leading receiver. Not bad for a guy nobody wanted.

"Give me guys like Rod anytime. Guys who are poor, smart, and hungry," Schlereth said. "Those are the guys who want it the most, and that's why Rod Smith has had one of the all-time great careers as a wide receiver in the NFL. He was our deep threat on our two championship teams, but he wasn't just a guy who sprinted down the sidelines and caught a ball now and then. He made big blocks, he was there in the trenches, in the tough plays. That's why he's a Hall of Fame player in my eyes."

## These Guys Made The NFL, And Now They Need Help

Craig Morton is politically conservative, the kind of guy who rolls his eyes on topics such as universal healthcare and the like.

So, it could be argued that his stance—that all former NFL players who played at least three years in the league deserve league-funded health insurance—is contradictory to his overall views. After all, why does a football player deserve guaranteed coverage over the average U.S. citizen who doesn't? Does a person who worked only three years in any organization deserve that organization's funded coverage for life?

Over lunch at a Berkeley, California, oceanside restaurant, Morton explains the difference:

"For one big thing, most of these guys get turned down for health insurance after they play football, even for a little while, because of 'pre-existing' conditions. They can't get it, not unless they pay extremely high, onerous premiums that many of them can't afford.

"A lot of these guys created the NFL, to what it is today, and I just think that the NFL should take care of them. Just for the humanity of it, the compassion of it. These guys are in dire need, and we should help them out. Why can't we give them health insurance? There's not that many of these guys anyway, it really wouldn't be a lot of money when you stack that up with all the money the league makes now."

NFL Players Association director Gene Upshaw has taken venomous criticism from many former players for what they call his neglect of their medical situations, and not doing more to address it. Former players such as Cardinals offensive lineman Conrad Dobler went public with their grievances, showing the extent of their physical conditions.

"To me, that's just horrible public relations for the league. You'd think they would be smarter than to want that to come out in the public domain. You'd think they would do more just on that fact alone. Even if their intentions weren't genuine and they only gave players health insurance to stop a bad headline from happening, that would still be fine with former players. These guys made the NFL, and now they need help. How much more money could that be? They could do that in a heartbeat. These are a minimal amount of players, I'm talking about, guys who were eight- or 10-year veterans. I don't think the guy who played one or two years should be included in that group. But the guys who played a while and helped make the league what it is today, these guys should get help."

## How To Be A Good Quarterback

If Craig Morton were coaching young quarterbacks today, this is what he would tell them:

Fundamentals, always. "Make young quarterbacks realize that, with the glory of the position comes the hardest work. If you're not willing to work hard at the fundamentals, you'll never be a great quarterback."

With mistakes, comes discipline. "I never once didn't make a mistake in practice in college. And so after every practice, I had to run ten 100-yard dashes. And I ran every one of them. Once you start hating mistakes, this will create less stress at important times. Once you start to really hate not doing things exactly right, only then do you start to finally do things right.

Sleep with the football. "Absolutely. Every quarterback should do that growing up. I did it. I slept with my baseball mitt and bat, too. When that football is always by you, though, or in your hands, it really makes a difference. You start to know everything about it, and it becomes almost like a friend, without sounding too goofy. But, trust me, it works."

Stay under center. "Young quarterbacks today are taught, in the spread offense, to make one or two reads and then take off running. There is no spread offense in pro football. There's a shotgun, but it was never a spread offense. To have a spread offense, you need to have a quarterback that is willing to go between the tackles. And in high school and college, you can have a guy like that. But when you get to the pros, you'll get killed doing that. I don't care how big or fast a young quarterback is, he'll get killed in the pros. So, a quarterback needs, I believe, to spend as much time under center as you can. That way, his eyes are concentrating downfield. But in the spread offense, the first thing a young quarterback does is look down at the ball. Your head should always been looking downfield, not down on the ground. Some people say, when you're in a shotgun, you get a better look at the defense, but not when the ball comes to you from the center. You're looking down at the ball, not the defense. For the mind to readjust, in just that one lost split second, makes a big difference. It puts you behind. When you're under center, you're looking at the defense all the time, and you don't have to refocus. When you get to the pros, by that time you know what a defense is doing better, especially when you're under center. You know where they're sneaking up. But, getting to that point takes an awful long time, and that's where all the other things beforehand come in, like getting those fundamentals down pat. You have to have that footwork down, the 1–2–3 drop, the 1–2–3–4–5 drop, or the 1–2–3–4–5–6–7 step, and you have to do them all the time, for different situations. The fundamentals that made me an NFL quarterback for 18 years are the same ones today that will take a guy to the pros. They never leave. But what's happened is there are these unbelievable athletes now, and too many coaches don't think they need the fundamentals as much. But that's a big mistake."

Break your pattern. "I always had these amazing arguments with Tom Landry in Dallas. He always said to a receiver, 'Never break your pattern.' And that was what a lot of coaches said, and still say. But I always argued the opposite. If a receiver notices a hole in a zone defense, he should be able to stop his pattern and look for the ball there, and the quarterback should be looking for that. But Tom just always said, 'Oh no, never break your pattern.' That was the history of football—you never break your pattern, even if they run two miles. But it doesn't have to be that hard, in a zone defense. On the Broncos, we had the same deal, not to break the pattern. But Haven Moses and I just did our own deals. He'd stop if he saw a zone, and I would find him. That's why we had such a good connection. We both could adjust, and would be on the lookout for it."

Don't be overcoached. "There's just no reason on earth why a coach needs to spend 12–14 hours a day making up game plans and plays, and subject his quarterback to that. Football always comes down to just a few plays anyway. Look at any great team, and they always just had a few plays they ran all the time. Why do you need to waste so much time going over other stuff that's not going to matter? Too many quarterbacks become overwhelmed with that extra stuff, and their careers suffer."

## Bad Apples, Dark Times, Stormy Moments

The Broncos have always had a good reputation as a franchise and in the Denver community. Countless numbers of players have done good works for the city, either through financial or human contributions, or both.

Not everybody was a saint, however.

Clarence Kay was a good tight end for the Broncos, playing from 1984 to 1992—one of the longer tenures for an offensive player in team history. He was a good blocker, and a reliable pass catcher. But the truth is, Kay's biggest headlines as a player were negative ones off the field.

Kay was arrested 12 times from 1984 to 2000, most for substance abuse, including cocaine. Several, however, were for domestic abuse and stalking. Probably the most serious charge came in April 2006, when he was arrested for slamming his girlfriend's head into a carport beam in Edgewater, Colorado.

Dale Carter is another player whose stay with the Broncos was marred by controversy off the field. Signed as a free agent from Kansas City in 1999 to a big $22 million, four-year contract, the star cornerback intercepted only two passes that season and the Denver defense allowed 318 points—the largest amount since 1995. When the 6–10 season finished, Carter failed an NFL drug test and was suspended the entire 2000 season. He never played for the Broncos again.

In the 2000s, the Broncos had a running back named Travis Henry who failed a drug test but avoided suspension, and fathered nine children out of wedlock with nine different mothers.

Star wide receiver Vance Johnson, one of the Three Amigos and one of John Elway's favorite targets in the 1980s and '90s, was involved in several off-field incidents, including arrests for domestic abuse and stalking. To his credit, however, Johnson turned his life around after that and became a good role model to kids.

As far as the toughest losses in Broncos history are concerned, other than the first four Super Bowl defeats, probably the worst was an AFC divisional playoff game on January 4, 1997, to the Jacksonville Jaguars at Mile High Stadium.

The Broncos came into the game after a 13–3 regular season, while Jacksonville was a recent expansion team. *Denver Post* columnist Woody Paige mocked Jacksonville in a game-day column, calling them the "Jagwads" and comparing them to a USFL team. Everything was going as planned, with Denver jumping out to a 12–0 lead.

But Jacksonville won, 30–27, behind the brilliant play of quarterback Mark Brunell. After the game, Jaguars coach Tom Coughlin, who would win a Super Bowl in 2008 with the New York Giants in another, well, giant upset over New England, publicly thanked Paige for firing up his team.

Paige, in a column titled "(D)isaster Day in Denver," wrote: "The columnist was unavailable for comment after the game."

But probably the darkest moment in team history, on or off the field, came on New Year's Eve, 2006, when young defensive back Darrent Williams was killed in a drive-by shooting after leaving a Denver nightclub.

The Broncos had already had a terrible day to that point, losing the final game of the regular season to a bad San Francisco team at Invesco Field at Mile High Stadium. A victory would have put Denver into the playoffs, but it didn't happen when the 49ers took a 26–23 overtime decision.

After the game, Williams and Broncos teammate Javon Walker went to a club called The Shelter. An aspiring music producer as well, Williams only went to the club because of promotional work that had been pre-arranged by a label he hoped to develop. Obviously, there wasn't much to celebrate, so the night ended shortly after midnight toasts were said, and Williams and Walker exited into a limousine.

But, beforehand, there was an apparent altercation between Williams and members of his party and unknown suspects. When

*A very promising and successful career and life was cut short on New Years Eve, 2006, when young defensive back Darrent Williams was gunned down outside a Denver area nightclub.*

Williams' Hummer limo took off, another sport utility vehicle followed. Someone fired 14 shots into the Hummer, one of which fatally struck Williams in the neck. He died in the arms of Walker, who was not hit.

The shooting stunned the city. Sentiment was well summed up by *Denver Post* columnist Mark Kiszla, who wrote: "Twenty-four hours before the death of Williams, the Broncos believed they were bound for the NFL playoffs. They will now be attending a funeral."

Bronco owner Pat Bowlen flew all players to Fort Worth, Texas, for Williams' funeral and established a memorial fund in his name.

"To lose a young player, and more important, a great young man such as Darrent Williams, is incomprehensible," Bowlen said. "To lose him in such a senseless manner as this is beyond words."

Walker was badly shaken by the death and, in 2007, he told HBO's *Real Sports* that he still keeps the bloodstained clothes worn that night as a reminder of his friend and teammate.

As of early 2008, no one had yet been apprehended for the shooting. In the "don't snitch" world of gangs, there was perceived fear or dishonor at coming forward. The vehicle the shots emanated from was impounded and registered to 28-year-old Brian Hicks, a member of the Crips gang. But Hicks was in prison at the time of the shooting, and none of his associates were charged with the crime. The case remains open.

## Under The Microscope

Morton wishes he made the kind of money players in the modern era make. But he does not envy the kind of media and public scrutiny they face today.

"To me, it would be absolutely foolish to put yourself in any kind of situation today, because you will be filmed by somebody. I'm amazed at some of the stuff I've seen athletes get accused of, or get themselves into. The biggest thing in our day was we were told to stay away from bars that might have mobsters in them.

Today, there are so many ways a pro athlete can be a target, from so many different types of unscrupulous people. They're making a lot of money, and that's always going to be a tempting target for others. I was never approached by a gambler. I'm sure the people they've gone to, they've known they were weak of character. Some of the things I've done, I probably would qualify for that. But I never did anything that jeopardized my team, in any way. There's just no way I would ever have been tempted by anything like that. But I can see how it might have happened more in the old days of sports. Players just weren't making the kind of money they make today. Guys don't need the money from doing anything like that."

## Pills Aplenty

The simple fact of pro football is that no player escapes the pain of the game. That's why teams have never been stingy with medication to dull as much of it for players as they can.

Morton said just about all of his teams had giant bottles of pills of various kinds out and available to all. Tylenol® "Number Threes," with codeine, were a popular pill, as were the occasional greenies to get pumped before a game.

"Sure, we had 'em. But I don't think a lot of guys really abused them really. Although, after I read Peter Gent's book *North Dallas Forty* and saw what some guys were taking, I thought, 'Shoot, I should have gotten my hands on some of that stuff!'"

## Memories, But No Memorabilia

For a guy who played 18 years in the NFL, one would think Morton would have an entire wing of his house containing nothing but memorabilia from his career. But step into the home of Morton and one finds very little of that.

"I gave everything away, to friends, coaches, and just anybody, really. All of the 20–something game balls I got in my career, I gave away. All the jerseys, all the equipment, everything. That's the way I wanted it. I mean, I might have something around here, but very little. Most people say 'what's wrong with you,' but that's just the way I am."

## Morton's Epiphany

Morton played his amazing 18 years in the NFL at the toughest position, but there was a moment early in his career where he knew he'd have to change or he'd never last.

"One game with Dallas, I went back to pass and had a big rush on me and I did something a quarterback is never supposed to do: I looked down on the field. I lost my discipline and just buried my head and looked at the ground, and that's the only time in my entire career that I could hear what was going on around me. I lost my focus on what I had to do, which is look downfield and make smart decisions. Instead, I looked down and heard what was going on and lost my head totally.

"I remember walking off the field and saying, 'Morton, you chickenshit. You had better never look down again, or you're not going to make it in this league.' And I never did that again. Not once in my career before or since did I ever hear the crowd or anything around me while I was playing. If you can hear the crowd, you're not doing what you should be doing."

## Don't Get Him Started...

Bring up the popular TV show *American Idol* or many of the reality shows of today, and you'll get a big grimace from Morton. To him, the mentality espoused in those programs is starting to creep into football, even at the high school and college levels.

"Everybody just wants the fame and the riches without having to pay your dues for it. You watch these shows like *American Idol*, and they just want to sing a couple songs and get famous right away from that. And they do! Everybody just wants a shortcut to success. You see it too much today in high school and college kids in athletics. Too many of them don't realize you have to work your ass off, day-in, day-out, to get good enough to play in the NFL or any other pro league. Maybe I'm just getting old and cranky, but I just see too much of a spoiled, indulgent attitude among today's kids. It doesn't happen overnight; its a lack of parental guidance and a personal sense of right and wrong."

## A Cowboy, Giant, or Bronco?

If Morton were inducted into the Pro Football Hall of Fame and, like baseball players, had to choose the one team to be shown on his plaque, which of his three NFL teams would it be?

"Boy, I'm going to have to take the fifth on that one. Nobody cherishes being a Denver Bronco more than I do, but I also played 10 years with the Cowboys. But I know I won't have to make that choice. Football doesn't require a player to choose one team.

"I can tell you one thing for sure, it wouldn't be as a Giant."

# chapter 8
# Retirement: New Adventures

*"Athletes always think it's going to go on forever. They're playing, they're making good money, they're famous—that's the way it is and that's the way it's going to stay. And, boy, I was like that too."*

—Craig Morton

## What Do I Do Now?

When a player's career ends, it's always traumatic to their life. Even the greatest players usually stumble around their first couple years of retirement.

When he called it quits in 1982, Morton was no different. He probably would have at least finished the season and maybe thought about playing beyond, if not for the players strike that forced a limited season.

Morton and striking teammates practiced in a Denver park, but it was a "joke," he said. When the strike was over, Morton's knees were no good anymore and he walked away with a limp.

"I had just figured out how to play the game and it was like, 'Hell, I've got to retire now.' I had just had my best statistical season ever, but I just couldn't do it anymore. The knees just wouldn't let me."

When there was no more structure of the daily life of a football player, Morton felt lost.

"I was always searching for something. I was just a screw up. I was restless and I just didn't have any purpose with what I wanted to do. I was just never really content about anything, always kind of anxious. And when you're not content about things, you do dumb stuff. That was me. All I can say is you learn from your mistakes and try not to make them again, and counsel those younger than you, like your kids, to avoid the ones you made. I hope they're a lot smarter—because of how dumb I was!"

## Morton and Money: Easy-Come, Easy-Go, and Lessons Learned

Pro athletes of the early days, of course, made a fraction of what most make today. As big as Morton's first deal was to him at the time, it was still 50 grand a year. That's a week's pay to many big-time athletes now.

Morton said players of his era were often caught in between with the money they made. It was more than the average Joe, for sure. But it wasn't enough to really be a Kingmaker in society, to really make the kinds of big-ticket purchases players today can make, like yachts, huge mansions, or major pieces of real estate. As a result, many players of that era were easy prey for investment scams. Players were always looking to turn their in-between money into something bigger through investments. Some worked, but many didn't, and Morton suffered through his share of bad deals that caused him financial problems after his playing career. So much so that he was forced into bankruptcy for a short time.

One of his worst deals was going into the restaurant business in Denver's Cherry Creek area in 1983, not long after he retired from the NFL. "Craig Morton's" lost a lot of the real Craig Morton's money, well over $100,000, and helped contribute to his declaring bankruptcy on October 19, 1990. He listed $1.1 million in liabilities, and $27,180 in assets.

"Going into that restaurant was a huge mistake. That damned restaurant caused a lot of pain to a lot of people. That was a tough deal. I didn't really want to be in the restaurant business, but my ego probably got the best of me. But it was just never a thing I would ever be good at. It just wasn't my personality to go around meeting people at tables every night. Then you get into bad habits. You start drinking. You have your own bar, so you sit and have a few cocktails and start letting all your friends come and drink and eat for free, and pretty soon you've given away all your profits for the night. Then, some of your employees don't show up, and you end up doing dishes at 3 in the morning. You start saying to yourself, 'How the hell did I get into this mess?' It's the hardest business there is. If you don't want to coach for 12 hours a day, then you certainly don't want to get into the restaurant business."

Morton doesn't make any excuses for his past financial problems. Today, he is happily solvent again, but offers up the dilemmas most players of his era faced:

"It was a lot of money to have, but it was not a lot of money to really do anything with. Basically, players of my era could buy a nice car, a nice little house, and a great steak dinner on the town. But you look at the superstars of today, where they have 25,000 square-foot houses, and 37 cars, and a few vacation houses in the south of France or whatever, and that's just something we couldn't do back then. In the past, the owners were the really rich ones. Today, the owners are still rich as hell, but so are the players. Most owners don't make a lot of money off their teams. They made it somewhere else and the team is a toy. And people forget, the taxes were higher back in my playing days. I don't know the exact number (the top bracket of the 1970s was up to 70 percent in most cases). You didn't have a lot of disposable income, really. It was always being taken away somehow. I did a little investing back then, and I did a little investing in real estate, and every time I lost my ass. And I had some people that really cheated my ass. But I wasn't very capable of saving money. And every time I tried to do the right things with my money—and I did, and I had some other good people around me who helped me try to do the right things with my money—there would always be a downturn in the economy. The thing I wished I had done was just cut off the payments for some of the things I invested in. But people would always say, 'No, it's going to turn, let's keep it going,' and I did, until I just ran out of money. And my pockets weren't that deep.

"And like I said, I got screwed by some people. I bought a lot of land in North Dallas when I played there, which would have seemed great. But the deal never got in my name, I found out. I was lied to by a guy advising me and whom I trusted. The only guy I ever helped put in jail was him.

"Athletes always think it's going to go on forever. They're playing, they're making good money, they're famous—that's the way it is and that's the way it's going to stay. And, boy, I was like that too. When I was playing, things were always great financially. I made a lot of money, had a lot of it coming in, and I just didn't think it would change. But most of my investments went to shit. But not all of them. When I played in Denver, I got to know a state senator named Arch Decker, and he got me to invest in a substance-abuse home, and we sold to a big conglomerate and made a lot of money on that. But then we got into the restaurant business—"Craig Morton's"—which was really a mistake. Then, I bought a lot of property in Denver, and the economy just went upside down. I put everything I had into it, and I just couldn't keep doing that anymore. It is what it is. Everytime I invested in real estate it went bottoms-up.

"I was just always a big spender when I went. Especially when I was with Denver. Some guys were a little tighter with a dollar, guys like Alzado. He wouldn't part with one very easily. But when I went out, I didn't really notice about other guys and their spending habits. I would just say, 'You're coming with me' and I'd take care of the check. I'm glad I did. That's just how I am. I don't regret it, but I wish I had probably thought out some better ways to make the most of my money. But there are just so many great things to invest in now, that we never had the opportunity to do. If you're a top draft pick now, in the first couple of rounds, there's no excuses now for not being financially secure. There are just too many things you can do with the money to be set up for life. I don't think that was the case when I played.

"Most guys worked off-season jobs when I played. I did some oil business stuff, and made some money doing it. A lot of guys sold insurance. I didn't do that, but I did lots of things. I've had several careers, I guess you could say. But nothing with quite the adrenaline rush of going back to pass in a National Football League game, with 275-pound men trying to take your head off."

## The Same Number, Retired Twice?

The Broncos are the only NFL team to have the same number retired twice—sort of. The number 7 is most widely remembered, of course, as the number of Hall of Fame member John Elway. But Morton also wore the number with the Broncos, although his first football card with Denver shows a different one. Today at Invesco Field in Mile High Stadium, both Morton's and Elway's names are on the Broncos' Ring of Fame, next to the No. 7.

Morton's '77 Topps card, however, shows him wearing the No. 5, which he never wore. Back in those days, players who were traded to a new team sometimes caught Topps off guard, because there were no pictures of the player in his new uniform. So, Topps artists would paint on a new uniform or helmet. They did a nice job on the Bronco orange, but got Morton's new number wrong.

Previously, Morton had always worn No. 14, with the Cowboys and No. 15 with the Giants because No. 14 was retired to the great Y.A. Tittle. So, why did he switch to No. 7?

"I always tell people it's because I thought I was half the quarterback I used to be. But really, the reason I took it was because in the Bible it says seven is the number of perfection. And I thought at that time in my life I needed something of that kind. So, it's a biblical number."

When Morton retired in 1982 and Elway came to Denver the next year, Elway informed the Broncos he wanted No. 7.

"So, (owner) Edgar Kaiser called me about that, and asked if it would be all right with me. That was a nice thing to do. But the first time I ever saw John Elway play football, I said right away, 'He's going to be in the Hall of Fame.' So, I told them it would be an honor to have that number go into the Hall on his shoulders, and I'm honored he would want it. And I was right."

When asked to name the greatest quarterback of all time, Morton doesn't take long to name the Duke of Denver.

"I don't know anybody who could do the things he did. I mean, from Unitas to Y.A. Tittle to Roger Staubach to Joe Montana—they just couldn't do the things Elway could. The reason why I think Elway is the best is that you could have put him on any team at all, no matter the talent around him, and he could probably still get that team to at least an 8–8 record. He was just so good that he could have won a lot of games by himself—and he did on some of those Bronco teams."

Another name Morton brings up, which might surprise some people, is Steve Young, the 49ers quarterback who was stuck in Montana's shadow early in his career.

"Some of the things Steve Young could do, nobody's going to be able to do that again because they'll get killed. The running part of his game, the anticipation he had, how smart he was—I think he's right up there with the greatest. Montana often gets mentioned at the greatest. He had the greatest offense in the world to run, and maybe nobody could run it like him. But if I had to take any quarterback in the world to win one game, I would take Elway."

## 13.6 Yards Per Pass

The above number is the average number of yards Craig Morton completed for each pass of his long career. When he retired, Morton ranked near the top of all quarterbacks for such an average. One of the first running backs to become almost as well known for his pass catching as his running was Minnesota's Chuck Foreman, in the 1970s. Otherwise, that wasn't the kind of thing coaches put into the game plan like they do today.

Tom Brady, for instance, averaged 12.1 yards per pass completion in his incredible 2007 season with the New England Patriots—a season in which he threw for a record 50 touchdowns and averaged 300.4 yards of passing per game.

"In Dallas, we had a lot of (short) patterns, but it was maximum protection on those plays. But, in Denver, I know we didn't have a lot of backs that caught passes. I would have loved to have had a back passing game, but it wasn't the case. In my era, if a play wasn't there, you just ate the ball or threw it away. And, running backs mostly just ran the ball and receivers caught the ball. That's the way the game was played a little more. Some teams had running backs more involved in the passing game, though, and some of those teams were very successful, like Dallas and Minnesota and Pittsburgh. But we won a lot of games the way we played, too."

## Coaching In The USFL

What were the odds of this?

In 1983, just a year removed from the NFL, Morton was hired as the new coach of the Denver Gold, in the fledgling United States Football League, receiving a two-year, $300,000 contract. Only, Morton wasn't the team's original head coach. Red Miller was.

After being fired by the Broncos, Miller was the choice of Gold owner Ron Blanding, a wealthy Denver real estate man. But Miller and Blanding didn't get along too well, mostly over monetary and personnel issues. Blanding held fast to the USFL blueprint of keeping player salaries low, to better keep ticket prices low for fans who wanted a springtime alternative to the NFL.

Blanding chose Morton as Miller's replacement, partly for marketing reasons. The Gold employed a lot of ex-Bronco players and coaches, and the team led the USFL in attendance (41,736) during the league's inaugural season at Mile High Stadium.

Still, how awkward was that, for Morton to replace his former coach? Five years before they were in a Super Bowl together, and now this.

"I was doing radio for ABC at the time, doing color commentary for USFL games. I did a couple of Gold games, and there were two guys who owned the L.A. Express, one of whom was a very good friend of mine, Alan Harmon, and the guy who started cable TV in Denver (Bill Daniels). When I first moved to Denver, Alan was my next-door neighbor and we were always close. He was good friends with Ron Blanding, and he told me that Blanding and Red weren't getting along too well. Alan asked me if I would ever be interested in coaching, and I said 'Well, yeah.' Not long after that, he said they were going to make a change with Red, and they wanted to know if I would want to interview for the job. I said, yeah, but I thought it was going to be a tough deal replacing Red. I didn't know if I was in favor of doing that, but I said I would talk to them. And the really ironic thing is that the guy who was going up against me for the job was Marv Levy, who was my college coach. So, it was between me and Marv, and they chose me, probably because I was the hometown guy. Marv took the Chicago Fire job. I didn't know I got the job with Denver until I got off a plane in Detroit, while I was on my way to do color for a game there on the radio. Ron Blanding gave me a very nice contract. In fact, they originally offered me $125K a year, and I said I'd take that, and Ron ended up increasing it to $150K.

"I don't think I talked to Red much at all, after I got the job. If we did, he would just be Red Miller and said, 'Good luck.' But I don't remember talking to him much. I inherited his whole staff when I took over, and they were not real happy about it. But I calmed their nerves. Only one guy quit, and we had a great staff."

Morton's tenure as Gold coach would prove to be a roller-coaster ride. He posted a 3–3 record to finish out the season replacing Miller, and got the Gold off to a fine 7–1 start the following season, 1984. That's when everything went to hell. Blanding sold the team for $10 million to Doug Spedding, a wealthy Denver car dealer. A Michigan native, Spedding liked hockey more than football, growing up idolizing Gordie Howe and the Detroit Red Wings. Before buying the Gold, Spedding owned the Colorado Flames of the Central Hockey League.

It didn't take long for Morton to know he wouldn't get along with Spedding. Spedding was a workaholic and wanted the same out of his coaching staff. Morton was not a coach who was going to take a sleeping bag to the office and spend all his waking hours watching game film. Things came to a head when Spedding went public over his dissatisfaction with Morton's work habits. In a *Denver Post* story, Spedding said, "I have never met a guy that works from 9 to 5 that could get it together." When the '84 season ended and the Gold narrowly missed the playoffs, Morton met with Spedding and it was mutually agreed there would be a parting of the ways. Morton received rest of his contract money, about $75,000.

"I wanted to quit right when Spedding was hired. I just knew it wasn't going to work with him. Our personalities did not match one bit. I knew that he didn't want me, too, and that he was trying to force me to quit. But I stubbornly said I wasn't going to do it, which was a mistake. And I probably sabotaged myself, because when he bought the team, I called the team together and basically told them, 'This guy is not a very nice guy.' It was like working at the car dealership under him. Everybody was a used-car salesman. We went 1–7 the rest of the year after he took over."

Morton was a laid-back coach, but not adverse to letting his players have it on occasion. He suspended cornerback and punt returner David Martin in the 1984 season, saying, "He's a detriment to our team right now, and has no place in this team's framework."

Martin did not go quietly into the night. He blasted back, telling the *Denver Post*, "I'm not going to walk around here all jolly and jovial like I'm happy with what's happening to me. (Bleep), I'm one of the lowest-paid guys on the team. I'm not going to be happy around here. I'm not going to be 'La-dee-dah, hey, everything's great.' You want me to go down and cover kickoffs—well, I'm not going to do that (bleep).... Now, all of a sudden, we lose a few games in a row and Morton's trying to put all the (bleeping) burden on me."

"That's why he wasn't playing that week," Morton says.

Morton can chuckle about that and the other many bad things that happened in the second half of the Gold's '84 season.

"It became pretty much an *Animal House* situation. The whole deal just collapsed after Spedding bought the team. But I'm not sitting here saying Craig Morton was all perfect and Doug Spedding was the entire reason that team went to hell. It was his team and he had every right to do whatever he wanted with it. I can't blame everything on him. But he was no Ron Blanding, I'll tell you that."

The USFL folded after the 1985 season. The league made the disastrous mistake of switching to a fall schedule, intending to go head-to-head against the NFL in 1986. Football fans in markets with two teams, such as Denver, not surprisingly chose the NFL. Spedding ended up filing a lawsuit against Blanding and the league, alleging everybody withheld information from him that the league was considering a move to a fall schedule the next year, and that he never would have bought the team if he'd known that.

But Spedding lost the case, partially over a Denver TV report three months before he bought the team that said, in fact, the USFL was considering a fall schedule the next year.

## Fun With George

The USFL was both a proving ground and a way station for head coaches. Some, such as Morton, got their starts coaching in the upstart league. Others, such as former Washington Redskins coach George Allen, rode out their final years there, mostly for the money. Morton (the laid-back coach and former quarterback of Allen's chief rival in his Washington years, in Dallas) did not get along at all with the workaholic, straight-laced Allen when they coached in the USFL.

Allen was a maniac for work, routinely sleeping in his office after a night of watching film. He supposedly ate a lot of peanut butter and ice cream because they were easy to eat quickly, allowing for more film work. He didn't drink or smoke, and was known as something of a prude, who didn't approve of scantily clad cheerleaders parading around his sacred sideline.

Morton played on the *North Dallas Forty* Cowboys teams and was never a stranger to a good time with the ladies, or a happening party. In a preseason 1984 USFL game between Morton's Gold and Allen's Arizona Wranglers, their two worldviews collided, in a heated and almost comical way.

"They came out to Denver, and we're both taking the field, and our girls are dancing and doing their thing and the music is blaring. Well, George gets really pissed off at me all of a sudden. 'What kind of organization are you running here?' he yells at me. 'This is a horrible thing! This is embarrassing!' So, he took his team to another field. He wouldn't even come out for the warm-ups. I told him, 'Come on out and enjoy this thing. This is good stuff!' Boy, he was pissed at me. Before the game, the coaches met with the game officials, and so we both had to be there for that. Well, this was really my first meeting with the game officials as a head coach, so I don't really know what's going on in that thing. George came up to me and put his arm around me and says, 'Craig, you know Tom—meaning Tom Landry—and I have gone through this many times, and things will be fine.' So, he starts talking to them and telling them all the rules he wants to be in place. And I really became very, very incensed about his whole patronization and just slighting me, that he was the great George Allen and we had no place being on the same field with him. I just said, 'Good enough George. We'll have a good time.' One thing he told the game officials was, 'We'll have no crackback blocks. So, I went to my team and said 'that son of a bitch, he's trying to invent rules for us, so here's what we're going to do: the first play, we crackback on his linebacker.' So we did, and he went absolutely berserk. He went crazy. We absolutely killed him in that game. We took his focus away from the game and onto things like that."

After that game, Morton was quoted in the papers calling Allen a, "Liar, cheat, and a thief." When it came time to play the Wranglers in the regular season, Morton was worried.

"I woke up that morning saying, 'Oh my god, what have I done? How do I back this up?' So I went to my team and I held up the headline and I said, 'What are you going to do about it?' and just walked off. When we played Arizona, I wore my raccoon coat, which pissed all the other coaches off. They were always giving me the finger over that. But we beat them again, because George was so pissed off about my coat. When we went down there to play them again later on, we had no chance. We were beaten bad, and they were ready for us. But I beat him twice. I psyched him out twice. I say that with pride! George was a good coach, but I always felt he was a little bit all hat and no cattle. His players loved him, but it was all about him in some ways. He was always in a limousine and thought he was better than everybody else. But you know what? He was still great for football. He was a character in that sense, and I always knew that. He was also a very good innovator, especially as a defensive coach. But I just had to play the only card I had against him, which was to psyche him out, and in my case it was (with) my cheerleaders and my raccoon coat."

## Other USFL Follies

The USFL's brief existence would no doubt make for a good book in itself. Colorful characters and stories abounded, including one involving John Hadl, who served as the Broncos' quarterbacks coach in 1983. The following year, Hadl coached the Los Angeles Express, which had a quarterback named Steve Young, who received a $40 million contract and continues to this day to receive $1 million annuity payments from the defunct team.

Hadl, who had a long career in the NFL as a quarterback, was smacked in the face by an Express player he had to cut.

"I remember we went out to the L.A. Coliseum to play them, and they had a huge crowd, partly because they hired Wayne Newton to sing at a postgame thing. Well, before the game, John has these huge sunglasses on and he took them off for a second and you could see this unbelievable black eye. I said, 'John, what the hell happened to you?' He said, 'Well, I got cold-cocked by a lineman who I cut.' He said that from now on, he was going to have his five or six biggest guys on his coaching staff stay around him when he had to make a cut."

Cutting a player, Morton said, "Was always a bad thing I had to do—but I didn't always do it; I'd have my player personnel director do it."

## Quarterback Coach: Experiment That Didn't Work

Six years after he retired from the Broncos, Morton was lured back to the organization in 1988 by Dan Reeves to serve as the quarterbacks coach. It turned out to be an awkward time for Morton, because he was the man in the middle of a feud between Reeves and star quarterback John Elway. Years later, Elway would call his time playing for Reeves "Hell." Reeves, never one to back down from a fight, countered, "Tell him it wasn't exactly Heaven for me either."

It didn't help that Elway suffered through one of the worst seasons of his career, and many fans took it out on Morton. A common theme on radio talk shows and in the papers became "Morton's screwing up Elway's game." The reality was that Morton had little input into much of anything under the hyper-controlling Reeves, and quit after one year.

"They wanted me to do some things, but then they wouldn't want me to do it. And, I'll never forget late in the year, when I really wasn't involved in too much, and I was feeling guilt about it. Because what happened was, after the preseason, Danny came up to me and said, basically, not to do any more with Elway, or not say anything more to him. I didn't know what that meant. So, I was just kind of a coach in limbo. And then one day, Elway came up to me and said, 'Learn the offense." And I said, 'John, I got nothing to do with anything.' I knew the offense from before, but I had no input into anything with the new one. When I coached Elway, all I really did was work on his setups and his feet. But Elway didn't have a very good year in '88, and everyone was booing me coming off the field. They thought I was responsible for how he was playing. But I just had very little to do with anything. It was an uncomfortable situation for me. John and Danny just never got along at all, and I could never really figure out why. But Danny was a quarterbacks coach before he came to Denver, don't forget, and he was Roger Staubach's quarterbacks coach one year in Dallas. He saw how Roger came a long way from where Elway was. Roger was a scrambler earlier in his career and he'd get out of the pocket a lot, but didn't start winning Super Bowls until he was more of a pocket passer, doing things on timing. I think he used that example of Roger to John, that Roger never became great until he changed some. And, really, that turned out to be true. When John started winning Super Bowls, he was more of a pocket passer. When he slowed down a little, when he wasn't as great a runner, it forced him to slow the game down a little. When the game slows down a little, you're a better player. And I'm sure John would say the same thing now."

Reeves said he thought Morton would excel as an assistant, but admits things just didn't work.

"Coming in as a coach, I knew the hours that it took to put in, to do the job," he said. "I don't think Craig had it in his mind, at that time, that coaching was what he really wanted to do with the rest of his life. We gave it a try, but in the end I think Craig wanted to be doing some other things, and I can understand that."

## Talk Show Host

In 1987, Morton was hired by Denver radio station KHOW to serve as a talk show co-host, with Barry Warner. While he had worked in radio as an analyst for USFL games following his retirement, Morton found the talk-show format to be ill-suited to his personality. He didn't last long at the job and was coaching with the Broncos a year later.

"It was laborious, I'll tell ya. It was late at night, and we didn't get a lot of calls. That's a tough job. I appreciate night-time radio talk-show hosts more than anything now. How do you get anybody to ever call? And the ones that do, it's the same ones every night. Barry was very good, but I wasn't very good. We talked about general sports, but I didn't do it every night, just a couple nights a week, and I still found that tough."

## Back To CAL-i

Morton was living in Arizona in the early 2000s, when his alma mater called about a job. Would he be interested working in the athletic department, helping to fund-raise for the school's many planned projects?

"I said I would be very interested. I had always wanted to go back home, so to speak. The only trouble was, they didn't have the seed money like they first thought for the position."

A bunch of former Cal football players heard about the funding problem and decided to lend a hand. These players were known as Pappy's Boys, those who played for legendary Cal football coach Lynn Pappy Waldorf, who coached Cal to 33 consecutive regular season wins from 1947 to 1950 and three Rose Bowl berths.

"Pappy's Boys said they would fund my position for a year. They did, and a year later the school funded the position (major gifts officer) full-time. So, it was just a great thing that happened to me, thanks in great part to those great guys. I was thinking about going back to Denver at the time and trying some things. But to be able to come back to the Bay area, there's just something to it. To me, it's home, and I don't want to be anywhere else but here."

On a sunny February, 2008, day at Skates by the Sea restaurant in Berkeley, it is easy to see why Morton would never want to leave. With a panoramic view of the Pacific and the San Francisco skyline in the background, an oceanfront table and a good glass of merlot, it doesn't get much better.

"Not bad, is it?" Morton says to a visitor from Denver. "You can see why this is one of my favorite places to come for a bite to eat and a cocktail sometimes."

# sources

## Books:

Frei, Terry. *77: Denver, The Broncos and a Coming of Age*. Taylor Trade, 2007.

Latimer, Clay. *John Elway: Armed and Dangerous*. Addax, 2002.

Little, Floyd and Tom Mackie. *Floyd Little's Tales from the Broncos Sidelines*. Sports Publishing, 2006.

## Websites:

www.pro-football-reference.com

www.www.nfl.com/superbowl

www.nfl.com